"Cultivating relationships through loving boundaries not only enriches friendships but also enables you to live a more stress-free life. *Drawing the Line* will be your go-to guide to getting started!"

Natalie Franke, author of *Built to Belong*

"*Drawing the Line* is a breath of fresh air for a tired mama's soul! Kate's refreshing advice is exactly what Christian moms need today. If you're craving deeper connection, faith, and happiness in a world that celebrates hustle and achievement at the cost of our sanity, then add *Drawing the Line* to your book list right away."

Emily Richett, founder of HAPPY PR and host of the *Amplify Show* podcast

"What a timely, eye-opening, and necessary message to women! I feel like Kate has been reading my diary! This book has been so helpful in teaching me to reconnect with my God-given intuition, set better boundaries, and step forward in life with confidence. Bravo, Kate!"

Polly Payne, mompreneur and founder of Horacio Printing

"In each chapter of *Drawing the Line*, Kate artfully guides us through the valleys of self-reflection, never leaving our side as we journey to the peak of reclaiming the life of our dreams. Through the doorway of deep discovery, this book brings us back to what matters most. It's elegant and grace-filled—a must-read for women seeking a more meaningful experience in their lives."

Amber Lilyestrom, author, keynote speaker, and acclaimed business mentor

"Kate's authenticity is breathtaking. This isn't someone who just talks the talk but someone who has walked the walk. She will guide you in creating the balance you need in work and in life."

Rachel C. Swanson, bestselling author and entrepreneur

"If you've ever found yourself burned out or feeling like you're hanging on by a thread, *Drawing the Line* will serve as a guide to help you cultivate a life of boundaries and balance. With a focus on the importance of alignment and sustainability, Kate beautifully articulates the true freedom and life-giving joy that can be found in setting boundaries and showing up for your own life in a way that creates longevity for those big, bold dreams in your heart versus allowing them to become a flash in the pan."

Kelsey Chapman, author of *What They Taught Me*

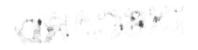

DRAWING THE
LINE

DRAWING THE
LINE

How to Achieve More Peace
and Less Burnout in Your Life

KATE CROCCO

BakerBooks
a division of Baker Publishing Group
Grand Rapids, Michigan

Published by Baker Books
a division of Baker Publishing Group
PO Box 6287, Grand Rapids, MI 49516-6287
www.bakerbooks.com

Printed in the United States of America

Library of Congress Cataloging-in-Publication Data
Names: Crocco, Kate, 1985– author.
Title: Drawing the line : how to achieve more peace and less burnout in your life / Kate Crocco.
Description: Grand Rapids, MI : Baker Books, a division of Baker Publishing Group, [2022]
Identifiers: LCCN 2021035428 | ISBN 9780801094774 (paperback) | ISBN 9781540902672 (casebound) | ISBN 9781493433964 (ebook)
Subjects: LCSH: Simplicity—Religious aspects—Christianity. | Self-actualization (Psychology)—Religious aspects—Christianity.
Classification: LCC BV4647.S48 C76 2022 | DDC 248.4—dc23
LC record available at https://lccn.loc.gov/2021035428

The author is represented by WordServe Literary Group (www.wordserveliterary. com).

Baker Publishing Group publications use paper produced from sustainable forestry practices and post-consumer waste whenever possible.

22 23 24 25 26 27 28   7 6 5 4 3 2 1

Annabelle, Charlotte and Drew.
Mommy loves you more than you'll ever know.
This book wouldn't have been birthed
if it weren't for you.

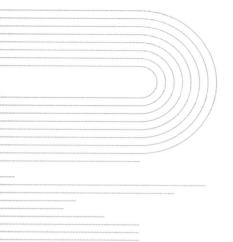

CONTENTS

INTRODUCTION

Building Our Foundation

A few years ago, as the December days grew colder and shorter, I found myself becoming unanchored. You might know the feeling: I was slowly slipping back into old behaviors that, in the past, had led to burnout. Exciting opportunities arose that I didn't want to pass up. Past perfectionistic patterns began to resurface, and I began working more than ever before. I was also nearing the launch of my very first book. It was a monumental moment—a lifelong dream. As I rocked my sixteen-month-old to sleep, I caught a glimpse of the swaddle hanging above her bookcase imprinted with an interpretation of Esther 4:14 that said, "Perhaps, this is the moment for which you have been created." At that moment, the pressure that had been building felt as though it might swallow me whole. I had no choice: I couldn't fail this book launch. I had two months to get this right, to do everything and anything under the sun to ensure that this book wouldn't go unnoticed in the world. This would be my one shot to spread my message of hope to the women who needed it most, and failure was not an option.

Have you ever felt pressure like this before? The feeling that maybe you've got one shot at something you've always dreamed of? Interviewing for the VP position you've been working toward since you started ten years ago. Driving to that first date after months of deep, connected phone conversations in hopes that maybe this will be the one. Being asked to speak at the next women's conference at your church to share your story of overcoming loss. These are the opportunities that we spend our lives waiting for, running them through our minds over and over again. These are also the opportunities that can throw our lives off-kilter. We become so consumed with having a positive outcome that we lose sight of the mystery in the journey, forgetting that God has predestined us for good no matter what our outcome is.

At the time, I felt immensely blessed. Not only was I launching my first book, but I was also writing my second, planning my first one-hundred-person live event, lining up dozens of podcast, radio, and print interviews, and launching another round of my business coaching mastermind program, all with just twenty childcare hours per week. But I was tired. I was running on adrenaline. And I had no idea how out of alignment I was about to become. I prayed that I could find a way to rest, disconnect from the pressures of work, and be more present for my family. I had created this business for myself so that I could intentionally live a life of alignment and enjoy my time with my family, not feel pulled in a million directions.

Maybe you're there today too, barely hanging on by a thread. Not only are you striving to nail that opportunity and make the next right decision, but you're also flooded with the pressure to impress your boss, be the best partner to your spouse, keep your kids' juice cups filled and diapers changed, provide top-notch services to your clients, remember not to lock the dog outside in the rain, keep in touch with your high school bestie, serve at church, and text your mom back.

I wish I could say that cultivating a life of alignment happened right away, that I magically woke up one day and had the instant drive to change, but the lessons our souls need most don't typically come that easily. They are most often solidified through intense pain and struggle. Let's just say that over the next couple of months, in conjunction with the pressure I was putting on myself professionally, family issues that were swallowing us whole, and a soon-to-be global pandemic, I was even slowly losing grip on my marriage. My out-of-control life was about to hit me head-on like a freight train, and all was about to come crumbling down.

I am writing this book because this is the book I needed a year ago. After nearly a decade of owning businesses, I had become really good at thinking like a boss. I mean, come on, that is the title of my first book! I had my mindset down pat in my business. I was impeccable at stating and claiming what I wanted, taking consistent action, and crushing my goals. I was no longer afraid of failure. I ran straight through rejection. My strategies had worked. Yet, I was beginning to struggle everywhere else.

In my first five years of business, I had become unhealthily wrapped up in my accomplishments and titles: Licensed Psychotherapist, Private Practitioner, Business Mindset

Coach—you get the picture. These titles were my identity, and it took almost losing my businesses multiple times for me to begin understanding that God had more for me than career success. I truly couldn't see beyond what was in front of me and never could have imagined having a life of fulfillment like I've been cultivating ever since. It feels like an honor (and a duty!) to share my story and journey with you today. To share how God knocked me off my feet (again) to show me what mattered most: my incredibly loving and patient husband; our two girls, Annabelle, three, and Charlotte (who we call Charlie), two; and our baby boy on the way.

I know many of you are struggling like I was. You have strived for perfection in all areas for so long, and you're just mentally spent. You live life going through the motions but aren't exactly sure why you're doing what you're doing or how you got there. You are tired and feel overcommited. You care so deeply about what others think of you, and you've neglected yourself to make them happy. You might not even know what you want out of life anymore. All that's clear is that you could use a nice nap or a weekend away, not with those you love most but by yourself. You desperately want to throw the phone across the room and never hear a notification ever again, yet you sit on the couch at night craving connection, feeling lonely.

You wonder if anyone else feels this way. From the looks of Instagram, you must be the only one. Everyone else seems to be able to handle career, family, friends, a Pinterest-perfect home, and gourmet meals. If they could look into your life, they'd see the dishes piled high, how you pick your outfit from a laundry basket full of unfolded (yet clean!) clothes each morning and pray no one notices the wrinkles, and those boxes you never unpacked from your move two years ago (true story) in the background of your Zoom calls. Why does it seem that everyone else has a picture-perfect life and you're just getting by? Oh, how you wish life could be simple and you could leisurely read, organize your home, sit and laugh with your hubby, and collect lightning bugs outside with your kiddos without feeling the pull to refresh your screen just *once* more to make sure no emails have gone unnoticed.

What if I told you that it's possible? That you can begin living a life of peace, simplicity, freedom, and abundance. Free from the pressure of missing the mark, passing over opportunity, failing the first time, or the dreaded FOMO. What if life could just feel like that four-letter *E* word that no one ever talks about? You know, *easy*? My husband used to cringe when I would say that word because even he didn't believe it could be possible in this lifetime. Let me just say that easy isn't a cop-out. It doesn't mean exempt from struggling or challenges but a mindset of growth. An intentional choice that life no longer has to feel hard and burdensome.

And you ask, "How can I begin? How can I step into alignment, build a life that no longer feels burdensome, create relationships that fill me up, and feel rested and 'at home' even when things are not going as planned?" Well, here is my answer: It all begins by drawing the line—setting boundaries and limits in any and every crevice of our lives. Alignment is born from knowing our own boundary lines and fiercely guarding them. Allowing anything to cross those boundary lines will inhibit you from living the life God has available for you, a life of holy fulfillment. I close my eyes to breathe in this passage:

> The LORD is my chosen portion and my cup;
> you hold my lot.

The lines have fallen for me in pleasant places;
indeed, I have a beautiful inheritance.
I bless the LORD who gives me counsel;
in the night also my heart instructs me.
I have set the LORD always before me;
because he is at my right hand, I shall not be
shaken.
Therefore my heart is glad, and my whole being
rejoices;
my flesh also dwells secure.
For you will not abandon my soul to Sheol,
or let your holy one see corruption.
You make known to me the path of life;
in your presence there is fullness of joy;
at your right hand are pleasures forevermore. (Ps.
16:5–11)

I believe this is God's beautiful definition of drawing the line: standing firm in our limits and stepping into the aligned lives he has available for us. Our lines or boundaries being set in pleasant places, a trust of God's great provision, a spiritual line connecting our hearts to God's truth, an unshakable faith, security in his plan and the path he has placed before us, fullness, joy, and even more than we can ever fathom. How beautiful is this? Is this not the best depiction of God's promise for you when you seek it?

Now, I'm sure you're wondering, "Now that I know that in order to live a more fulfilled life I have to find this so-called place of alignment, how do I do it? How do I really grasp and conceptualize alignment? How long will it take me to get there? How will I know when I reach it? Does it change? How will I know if I am out of it?"

Let's begin with good old *Merriam-Webster*. Here is the full definition of *alignment*:

1. the act of aligning or state of being aligned especially: the proper positioning or state of adjustment of parts (as of a mechanical or electronic device) in relation to each other
2. a: a forming in line + b: the line thus formed
3. the ground plan (as of a railroad or highway) in distinction from the profile
4. an arrangement of groups or forces in relation to one another[1]

So first, *alignment* means the proper positioning of something. For example, when putting together Ikea furniture and two boards don't quite line up, the screw will not make it through the two holes. When circumstances are properly positioned, alignment is present.

Second, it literally means the physical formation or drawing of a line. Where there is a line drawn, there are also rules made. Do not cross over the double yellow line. Please stand behind the red tape until we call your name. This state line dictates which laws are in place. We so often have to set clear lines with those we communicate with in order for us to feel at peace.

Third, *alignment* means a road map to follow. Stay within this plan in order to reach your destination. When we swerve outside of God's plan for our lives, we go off track and out of alignment.

1. *Merriam-Webster*, s.v. "alignment (*n*.)," accessed August 17, 2021, https://www.merriam-webster.com/dictionary/alignment.

And last, it means the arrangement of groups or focus in relation to one another, meaning follow these guidelines for success.

Now think about examples of when things physically or metaphorically felt out of alignment for you. When you tweaked your neck at the gym and couldn't work out for a week without being in excruciating pain. Or when your tires were out of alignment and your car wasn't driving smoothly. Or how painful it felt when your line (boundary) was overstepped by a coworker. Or when you could sense in your spirit that something in a particular situation just felt off. We are faced with instances involving alignment each and every day, yet because alignment is not visible to the naked eye but a self-measured feeling, it is easily overlooked until something is completely off-kilter. Little by little, lines are crossed, conditions are blurred, situations snowball, and "out of nowhere," we are hit at full impact. Just like that cold December when I was slipping out of alignment. I was in denial but about to be hit hard with the truth.

Can you identify with my story? Maybe you felt as though you were in alignment, but then you were knocked down. Do you have a clear picture of what true alignment could look like for you? I think it's important before we go any further that you get a glimpse of what is possible for your life. When I hear the word *alignment*, some things that come to mind for me are being more patient with myself, playing princesses with my girls free from the pressure of needing to be productive, speaking truth to those I love without sugarcoating anything, saying no way more than saying yes, having margin in my schedule to sit and read a book with a hot cup of tea while petting my dog, being open to conversation with a stranger after yoga class, having time to write and mail a handwritten letter, not checking the time every twenty minutes, breathing and no longer holding my breath, and the best of all, starting my day in the Word with Jesus. We all desire to have what alignment ultimately delivers, which is greater peace, fulfillment, and intentionality.

Alignment for you today may look entirely different from what I describe as a slow and intentional life. Alignment for you may look more adventurous and have more movement and curiosity in it. No one way or another is wrong, and alignment will shift for each of us with the shifting of life's seasons. So take a moment to sit, visualize, and meditate on the Scripture passage I quoted earlier. Close your eyes and slowly breathe in. Envision how different your day-to-day could be if you could infuse even just a bit of this passage into your future steps.

What felt aligned for you three years ago when you took that dream position at work may today feel like the completely wrong path. As we grow and stretch and reach goals, our barometers will shift. As we experience pain, as we uncover truth, as we better understand who God says we are, our barometers will also shift. Throughout this book, I will be sharing some very personal examples of how alignment has shifted for me throughout the years and the sort of power struggle I've had with it at times to keep myself feeling safe and comfortable. Bottom line: As humans, we despise change. We are creatures of habit, and once we settle into that new job or come up with a new sleep schedule for our kiddos or have a recurring date on the calendar with our childhood girlfriends, we want things to stay the same. But things never stay the same. We grow, our kids grow, our perspectives shift, people change, we uncover new revelations, life happens, and often we are left with less time. Whatever the shift may be, it's inevitable that some shift will happen. What felt like confident, aligned choices yesterday are not bound to feel the same tomorrow.

So now that we know alignment is ever changing, how do we know when we are no longer in it? Misalignment just plainly looks like the opposite of alignment. I can sense that I'm out of alignment when I am not finding joy and comfort in the little things. Life feels like going from point A to point B with zero margin. I slowly slip out of healthy habits and priorities to tend to fires. I fall asleep in front of the TV watching something to pass the time rather than filling my soul with a good book. I no longer set up my coffee maker at night and go to bed a bit earlier so that I can get up at 5 a.m. to read the Word, write, work on my other passion projects, or just have my coffee while it's still hot and in silence before the kiddos begin calling for me. These examples are huge indicators of where I am at in life. Another clear indicator that I am slipping out of alignment is when I try everything I can to force something to work and it won't budge, whether it's a friendship I should let go of or a project that has me hitting a wall. Recently, it's been a season of trying to do it all as a mama—full-time work-from-home job, full-time homeschooling—and realizing one of these has to give.

It really is hard to feel like you're giving up on a dream. But do you know what's even harder? Waking up one day and realizing that this thing you've been forcing has been out of alignment for ten years and that life would have been a lot easier if you had just trusted that God's plan is always better than yours. Do yourself a favor and write this verse somewhere handy, as I know you'll be coming back to it in the future: "'For I know the plans I have for you,' declares the LORD, 'plans to prosper you and not to harm you, plans to give you hope and a future'" (Jer. 29:11 NIV). In the coming chapters, I'll be sharing stories of when it felt as though my dreams were being stripped away, but little did I know they were being replaced with something better. God's plans are always better than ours.

So how will you know when you are in alignment? We know what it is, we know what it isn't, but how can we clearly identify when we are living in it? Well, let's just say this. I've wanted to write a book about alignment for years, yet I could never clearly communicate the steps it would take to reach this level of living. Looking back, it all makes complete sense. Although many times I felt I was in alignment, I hadn't truly experienced it enough to really grasp the fullness of it. Alignment is really hard to quantify, and as humans, we want clear, concise steps, road maps, equations, or blueprints to follow to get results. We are also extremely impatient and at times reach levels of resistance because we haven't accepted that what we so badly desire isn't for us just yet. Oh, that sentence stung as I wrote it. I can't tell you how many times I tried to force things into existence rather than wait my turn. And alignment, friend, is something that cannot be forced.

So the short answer to what is a rather long question and will take an entire book to answer is this: You will 100 percent know you are in alignment when, even if life is hard or devastating, your hope in Jesus is not shaken. You know that despite the grief, loss, uncertainty, or whatever you are facing, he hasn't left your side for one minute. You may want to throw in the towel and doubt his plan, but you know that you will be okay in time, and if you're not okay, he is still working.

As I write this, my life is far from perfect. There are loads of uncertainty with our economy and the future of the businesses we are juggling. Friends around us are dealing with health issues. There is political and social unrest. I am in complete denial that we are welcoming another human into the world and will have three babies four and under. Yet, I am more confident than ever that my God is good and my God is in control. I know there is the possibility that everything can come crashing down around me at any time, yet I have an inner peace that God is always working things out for the good of those who love him (Rom. 8:28). You may have never felt a peace like this before, and guess what? That's okay. We will get you there, sister. Yes, it will take some hard work— such as chipping away at outdated beliefs no longer serving you, learning new skills and behavior modifications, learning to work with (and not against) your feminine tendencies, and potentially seeking some professional help. Despite the discomfort, when we are finished, I can assure you that you will begin experiencing ease.

Before we get started, I want to celebrate the fact that you are reading this book. You are probably in a place of knowing something has to change. You know that God has a plan for you and that God's desire for you isn't for life to feel as daunting as it has felt. Maybe you have everything you've ever asked God for in your hands today, but more than ever before, you feel depleted and unfulfilled and just crave peace, stillness, simplicity, and wholeness. No matter how much you have, you can't seem to shake the feeling that you haven't quite reached where you want to be. You are only desiring more and then striving more.

Well, first of all, know today that you are not alone. Our world has become so cluttered with bigger, better, louder, faster, and it's taken a toll not just on you but on others as well, including myself. Even therapists struggle—we are human, after all! And you know what has helped tremendously in my journey to alignment? Allowing vulnerability to permeate my life. Not being afraid to share what's true for me today and what no longer feels true for me tomorrow. We have been conditioned to act as if we have it all together, to never show weakness, to pretend everything is okay, and it's slowly hurting our connection with each other. I've been there. "Therapists should have it all figured out. Therapists should never appear to struggle. Therapists should be the shining example of how to cope during tragedy." I have had much more success helping women find their true calling and step into alignment now that I have gone against the grain, allowed vulnerability to take over, and bared it all. I know you might not be ready to let your guard down just yet. That's okay. This is a beautiful journey that will forever be evolving as long as you are living and breathing.

So moving forward, I am going to help you find alignment by showing you how to do the following:

- Uncover, state, claim, and then draw your lines.
- Quiet the noise around you while turning up the dial to hear God's voice.
- Discern God's truth from the world's truth.
- Uncover your deepest desires and create an unshakable belief in those dreams.

- No longer allow disappointment to shake you by detaching from outcomes.
- Identify prideful or self-motivated places and lay them down.
- Become even more connected with your gut instinct.
- Ask for forgiveness rather than permission.
- Accept that you have a choice and life can be easy.
- Clear the physical and metaphysical clutter that adds weight to your life.

Are you ready? Grab hold of my hand. I've got you, sister. This will not be an easy ride, but I can assure you that new life and revelations will be born out of it.

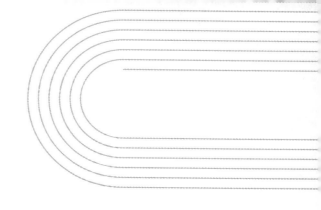

CHAPTER 1

Never Say Never

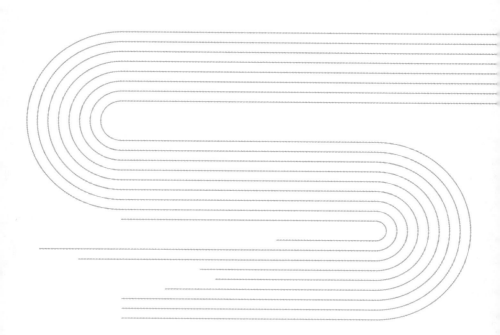

You know what's really painful? Being completely sure of something, maybe even having a pretty public stance on it, and then realizing that your belief or decision is no longer in alignment with your life and values. Holding on too tightly to what once was can really hold us back from living out God's fullness for our lives. I bet some of you are living through this internal struggle today—doing all you can not to cave and change your mind about something that once felt so right for you.

I had spent two years anticipating February 2020. I had engaged in conversation after conversation with family, friends, mentors, business besties, my Bible study group, and most of all my public social media community. We would be enrolling our girls in full-time day care so that I would have the space to really dive back into my career and everything that comes with the launch of a first book. Up until this point, I had been scrappily working with whatever bread crumbs of time I could find outside the part-time childcare hours we had. As much as I loved my girls, I really wanted my career back too. Of course, nothing crazy like before, but just enough to build the momentum again. Pre-kids, I was known for working seventy-plus-hour weeks in my businesses. I had also worked very hard to get back to a mindset of "I can still be a good mom even if I allow others to watch my children so that I can focus on my dreams." That department was a tough one, and I was still a pretty newish mom at this point. Life was a whirlwind the first two years of motherhood, finding out we were having our second baby when our first was just nine months old and I was in the midst of full-fledged breastfeeding and raging hormones.

That February, the girls fifteen months and two and a half years old, I remember dropping by my parents' and them casually asking if we had begun to think about schools for the girls. I literally was just trying to launch a book and get them out of diapers first, but I guess that's what responsible adults do—plan ahead. And so, of course, I answered with, "Um, not a clue. We will think about it once they're both out of diapers." But then my father offered an idea that he thought was brilliant: the *H* word. You know the thing that all the perfect moms do who devote their lives to the good of their children. Homeschooling. I almost spit out my water. *Me? Homeschool? You mean us living on a prairie, wearing matching hand-sewn dresses with Laura Ingalls Wilder braids, baking homemade bread, writing on chalkboard tablets?* I chuckled. "No way would I ever want to do that," I said under my breath. I pushed the stroller home that day, particularly irked that my father would even offer such a piece of advice. If anything, I could see us someday traveling around the world during their school breaks so that I could speak to groups of women. But stay home all day long with nowhere to go? That would literally be my worst nightmare.

Before we move into the nitty-gritty of alignment in this book, it's crucial that we get everything out on the table by focusing on three very important things. First, in order to step into the fullness and abundance that is available to us in life, we have to get vulnerable. We need to admit what feels uncomfortable to us. And sometimes we also have to release our pride. Vulnerability and pride are like oil and water—they just don't mix. Second, we need to develop an awareness of the emotions that certain phrases and comments bring up for us. It's important that we become aware of what irks us, like the homeschooling comment my dad casually brought up, and get comfortable sitting with these feelings and unpacking where they are coming from. And third, we need to develop flexibility in our thinking. As the title of this chapter states, "Never Say Never," it is important that we release absolutes in order to open ourselves up fully to opportunities that we may have once rejected but are really for us. Before we dive in, I am going to leave you with a verse to read out loud and meditate on. I want you to ask God to soften your heart, help you let down your guard, and open you up to flexible thinking and discernment.

Do not be conformed to this world, but be transformed by the renewal of your mind, that by testing you may discern what is the will of God, what is good and acceptable and perfect. (Rom. 12:2)

Shedding Our Pride

We are going to be spending quite a bit of time together throughout these eight chapters. I'm also going to be getting pretty vulnerable with you because I know how impactful our stories can be on others. So can you do me a favor? I can't actually hear you, but can you hold yourself accountable to really do this work? I always say, "Don't waste what is in your hands," so if you are going to read this book, do it wholeheartedly, immersing yourself in every page so that you can walk away with zero regrets rather than wishing you had paid a little more attention or practiced better intentionality. We will get into intentionality later in the book, but for now, just get honest with yourself in terms of pride. How is pride currently keeping you from living the abundant life God has for you? Are you struggling to apologize to your best friend after a misunderstanding? Are you having difficulty asking for help at your job because you're afraid your boss will think you're incapable of doing the work? Are you still in that volunteer position at your kids' school not because you have the time or necessarily want to volunteer but because you're afraid the other moms will think you're a quitter? Get honest. We all have something we are doing that isn't serving us, that is holding us back from living in full alignment, but that we continue to do because of our ugly pride.

Well, envision this. How would it feel to admit whatever it is you're hiding and just speak the truth? Yes, this might ruffle some feathers, cause some people to feel angry or frustrated with you, maybe even push a loved one completely away for the time being, but, ultimately, the truth always wins. Maybe you're like me and the person you are about to set off is actually yourself. You swore you would never believe or do a specific list of things, and now you've changed your mind, caught yourself red-handed, and are doing them.

Before we get started, it's important we lean in to the power of being vulnerable. What does pride feel like inside? Pride feels like constant pressure and resistance, and when you carry it, you are on edge, tense, ready to fight and defend, and you have a closed stance and a closed mind. When you are vulnerable, you experience fullness and freedom. You are confident speaking your mind and feel as though you are no longer hiding or keeping secrets. You are inviting of conversation that includes differing opinions, and you are open to what's to come next. Which way would you prefer to live? I know I would choose the second, hands down. However, pride can easily weasel its way back in at any time, so we need to intentionally practice vulnerability. Practicing at all times in the little things will prepare you for the things that feel much harder to stomach in the future.

So let's go back to me taking offense to the suggestion of homeschooling. The year 2020 was when everything I had not just asked but begged God for was now in my hands. I had such high hopes for all I would accomplish in my writing and coaching career. I felt unstoppable and firmly rooted in making my goals a reality. Then in early March, three weeks into my kiddos now having full-time day care and my book launch, something shook not only our world but also my pride and my strategic plan. A mysterious virus called COVID-19 hit our country, and no one really knew what to do, leaving us all panicked. We were living in New York, and so our city was one of the first to experience a mandatory lockdown. So, um, yeah, that meant my worst nightmare was about to play out: everyone home, under the same roof, 24/7 for six weeks, which at the time I had no idea would turn out to be months. What did I do to deserve this jinx? Was this a self-fulfilling prophecy? Okay, in all seriousness, this was not about me. Families were clearly suffering—caring for sick loved ones and suffering loss, experiencing jobs being stripped away, and missing weddings, birthday celebrations, and even funerals. Everything that once seemed so secure no longer was.

My kiddos were not yet of school age, so instead of experiencing what I thought would be my big break, I laid down my career yet again to be the 2020 version of June Cleaver. And let's just say I didn't take this so gracefully—my pride was hurting big-time. And what does pride do? Pride eggs us on to kick and scream and hold on tightly to things that are no longer ours or that are no longer aligned with our life vision until we slowly can't hold on any longer, lose grip, and watch what we were holding on to slip right out of our hands. You will hear me say this many times. One thing I am sure of is that God will always give us what we *need*, not necessarily what we *want*. I so love Isaiah 55:8–9, which says, "My plans aren't your plans, nor are your ways my ways, says the LORD. Just as the heavens are higher than the earth, so are my ways higher than your ways, and my plans than your plans" (CEB). Even though we can conceptualize this, it's still not easy to accept that what we want is not always what God has planned for our lives. And to fully live out his promise for us, we have to set pride aside, begin living with an open heart and open hands, be ready and willing to lay down our egos, and take on what his plan is for us.

The year 2020 was a test for pretty much everyone. It was the year when many things became clear. Family members were forced to face one another every waking minute of the day, and those living alone were faced with the loudness of their internal dialogue 24/7. Big, grand plans were stripped away from us. This was a recipe for disaster, but also an opportunity for self-discovery, with new truths being uncovered. Being locked inside, left to face myself, my feelings, and my family, I was met with a deeper truth, insight, and 20/20 vision. I began to see God soften my heart, strip me of my self-centered career plans, and call me to quit chasing all that I had been wanting. I felt him calling me to, quite honestly, the opposite of what I had prayed for. I had wanted opportunities to speak and use my voice in the business world *outside* the home, but instead he was calling me to stay planted and use my voice *within* my home. Yet, I resisted. My pride told me, "I can still do it all. Even with kids home, I'll figure it out. I always do. I can't fail my first book launch. I need to get my voice out there so I can make an impact in this world." And so, even in the midst of a global pandemic, my pride convinced me that I could still make this grand plan happen, until God showed me who was really in charge. I mean, come on, we ultimately know it's always his way or the highway.

When I tried to force something, each time he responded with a subtle, "I told you so. Just stop already." Here are a few examples. Waking up at 3:30 a.m. to film videos and then losing them. Scheduling podcast interviews for 9 p.m. when the kids *should* be fast asleep but the dog had a barking fit at a leaf blowing in the wind in the backyard resulting in awake and screaming children. My husband having an emergency work meeting that needed to be kid-free when I was scheduled to present a training. You get the picture. I was forcing something that God was trying to show me was no longer lining up with his plan for me. In that moment, I clearly felt him impressing on my heart these words: "Kate, these gifts are all for you, but not for you right now. Don't force what you can't control. Embrace this season with your small children home with you. Focus on only the present and stop trying to strategize how to make this all work. Just be still and let me do the work for you." Ouch, that was hard to hear. I wasn't ready to have to be flexible again. I wanted things my way—my very specific plans.

But it was a wake-up call and very clearly revealed that I was forcing life to happen. I was no longer living in alignment—a life of provision, a full heart, an unshakable faith, security in his plan and the path he has placed me on, fullness, joy, and peace. I wasn't experiencing any of this, had quickly lost my grip, and was now feeling lost. Life felt really hard. Everything was an uphill battle. I needed to release my pride, quit the inflexible thinking, and begin leaning in to his direction again. And so the journey of getting back into alignment began.

What are you pridefully holding on to today that you sense God is trying to tell you to release? Maybe you're in a place similar to the place I was in, having big, grand plans but sensing him telling you to lay those plans down. Maybe it is a failed business you swore you'd never give up on. You did everything you could to make the business work, but for some reason, you sense God trying to show you that it's no longer for you. Or maybe like me you scoffed at the idea of homeschooling, but you sense that home is where God wants your family in this season. It's crucial that we tune in to his still and steady voice, release the chains that have kept us captive, and surrender to him. When day care reopened six weeks after lockdown but I felt God impress on my heart not to send the kiddos back, I thought maybe I was losing my mind. It didn't make sense, but I was confident that I felt the call to keep them home, which was the opposite of what

I had wanted just six weeks prior. My pride made keeping them home a tough decision, but I knew without a shadow of a doubt that it was the right decision. Did it sting my pride? You bet it did, but being vulnerable will soften your heart as well.

Living with pride is lonely. In order to step into a full and abundant life, we need to get vulnerable. We need to admit that what was once for us is no longer for us. We need to release the pressure we put on ourselves to woman up, to stick with it, to not be a quitter and lay it down at the feet of our Father. You know that relief you feel when you apologize after a nasty fight with your partner? How you feel when you confess that you were being slightly stubborn saying his home decorating taste was lame and not letting him put up the baseball poster you caught him attempting to hang in his office and that how you think it looks really doesn't matter in the grand scheme of things? Tiny example, but when we can surrender, lay aside our pride, and be vulnerable to receiving feedback or criticism, that's when fullness is able to flow into our lives. It certainly stings hearing your partner call you controlling over a silly baseball poster, but it's also freeing when you can set your own stuff aside, admit that maybe you blew it out of proportion, and accept the truth—that in the grand scheme of things, the poster is not going to harm anyone.

Tuning In to What Irks Us

Something I've learned over the last few years is to pay close attention when something triggers or stirs an out-of-proportion reaction in me, because it's usually not for nothing. When we can remain confidently detached from a comment, interaction, or situation, it's typically a sign that it has very little to no power over us. Here's an illustration. I drive a Ford F-150, and for those of you who are not familiar, it's a very large truck! We have it because it fits all the kids and does double duty as a construction vehicle for our income properties. Quite often when people see me driving it or it comes up in conversation, they will say something like, "Wow, that truck is huge!" Well, guess what? I have zero connection to that comment and couldn't care less whether they say my mode of transportation is big, small, old, or new—I just really don't care. On the other hand, something else that's huge and has been commented on that does stir up emotion for me is my pregnant belly. I'm not a very large person to begin with, but when pregnant, I tend to carry quite heavily in the belly region. And not *if* but *when* people comment on the largeness of my belly, unlike the truck comment, it does stir something up for me. Deep down it hits a nerve because it has emotional attachment—going way back to my history of an eating disorder and a fear of being seen as "big." See the difference?

So as you're on this path to living a more honest, open, full, and intentional life, it's important that you don't discount when feelings are triggered and surface. We have to allow ourselves to sit with our feelings and process our thoughts about them. Here are two questions to help you. First, can you sense why a comment or experience is bothering you? And second, is your pride attaching this comment or experience to a past story? Going back to the homeschool comment, it brought to my mind, "Good moms dedicate their lives to raising their children; therefore, homeschooling would make me a good mom." But then on the flip side, what it also brought up was ego. "But I worked so hard to get to where I am in my career. I can't fail my launch plan. I'll be disappointing others who are counting on me. And will I look like a failure or that I don't care about my career if I were to take time off to be home with my kids? After all this work I've done, how will others perceive me?" And still, part of me did want to spend more time with my kiddos. I think no matter where you are in life, part of you always slightly aches for the thing you did not choose.

In most instances, fixed, inflexible thinking or pride will always end up winning unless we work hard at making a conscious effort to avoid it. My vision was so murky that I saw career success and financially providing for my family as what would bring me fulfillment. And my ego wanted that to be true. However, when I sensed that weird tension come up with that comment, I knew there was more to it. So I tuned out the noise, got vulnerable, and allowed the Holy Spirit to show me that I was making career choices not from a place of freedom but from a place of not wanting others to view me as a failure. And that was not easy to take, especially as I wasn't so willing to lay down my career plans that quickly. I had to experience the resistance as I fought it for some time before I was willing to fully surrender. Let's get real. I pretty much didn't have a choice. Sometimes this is the only way God can elicit change in us—to pretty much strip us of what we have, what makes up our egos, until we have no other choice but to surrender and lay it all down at his feet. But when we arrive at this place, surrender, acknowledge our pride or inflexible thinking, and then commit to starting over, that's when life begins to feel easier. This is where all the pieces fall into place and peace and fulfillment are found.

Where in your life are you sensing buttons being pushed and nudges being made? What have you heard someone say or what has directly been said to you recently (maybe in the last year) that you haven't been able to shake? Take some time to write it down, pray about it, and ask God to reveal to you what he is trying to show you. Ask him to shine a light on any parts of you that are being led by ego rather than by him.

There Are No Signed Contracts

Alignment is like the wind; it has permission to change at any time. What felt 100 percent right for you in the morning can quickly shift and no longer be in alignment for you by evening. When uncovering what a life of abundance looks like, keep in mind there are no signed contracts—you have permission to change your mind at any time. When we can learn to embrace flexibility and release black-and-white thinking or absolutes, we can more easily step into God's calling for our lives.

Something that is really important to note is that we cannot even fathom the depths of what God has available for us. As humans, we naturally limit God's giving capabilities. Our mindsets hang out at the level of abundance we are capable of envisioning and then receiving. But God says, "I have so much more for you if you would just let go of what once was." What I had trouble grasping during the start of the pandemic was that something that was once so clear to me, a focus on my career, could still be available to me in an even better way than I was trying to force. I viewed having kiddos home with me as only a limitation to or a failure in my career. But what God was trying to show me was that by releasing this very singular dream, I could open the flood-gates to an even better dream and take on a new lifestyle of intentionality that I never saw possible. He began to reveal to me that I was even more capable of handling career, kids, and homeschooling than I thought I was. And because I invited flexibility into my thought pattern and surrendered my pride and career (for the moment), God blessed me and revealed a simpler way to live. Because I was willing to embrace flexibility and lay down my prized possession for a season, he gave me what I really needed.

I think back to Abraham in the Bible (Gen. 22). My situation was minuscule compared to his, but both portray on different levels the theme of trust and what's available to us when we honor God in hard choices. Abraham was one hundred years old before his wife was able to conceive. And when Abraham had what he had waited so patiently for, his son Isaac, God asked him to lay this dream down and sacrifice his son. Abraham was a wise man who trusted God through the years of waiting and knew that if he was obedient, God would come through yet again. Abraham was willing to be obedient and lay down the biggest gift in his life to show his devotion because of his unshakable faith and his flexible thinking. But ultimately, he knew that God's plans are always higher and more intricate than ours and that God would not let him down. We too, like Abraham, need to be able to see the bigger picture. As we learned earlier, inflexible thinking or pride can hold us back from God's ultimate plan for our lives. But when we live in full surrender and truly believe that God will work all things out for the good of those who love him, we can more easily give up what once was for what God has for us.

Something we are taught as young kids is to always keep our word. We fear that if we agree to something and then go back on it, we are lying or just plain not being a good person. We obviously teach kids this because we want them to be truthful, loyal, and not flaky. However, as adults, when we can see the bigger picture, at times it's important that we detach from that rule to do what is right. Many years ago, after staying home with my firstborn and struggling to get back to work and create traction in my business, I swore I'd never leave my career again to stay home. I could have easily allowed my pride to hold me back from doing the right thing and used the excuse "I should stick to my word." But then I would not have lived out God's plan for me to experience a greater level of peace, joy, and abundance. When we can release our pride to be right or release the pressure to do what we think is right in certain instances, God can fully open doors for us to live out the lives he has called us to live.

Letting Go of What Once Was

So as we wrap up this chapter, I want to leave you with a little road map that you can keep handy for when you are at a crossroads and are struggling to let go of what once was and accept the new so that you can receive God's full abundance for your life. Go through the questions one by one, journal, process what feelings surface for you, and talk with God. Have a candid conversation and ask him to reveal to you the right next steps to take.

1. First, examine the situation you are in and ask yourself if you have a strong aversion to the thought of letting go of what once was for something you maybe said you would never do. When someone brings it up or it naturally hits your mind, does it sting a lot?

2. Then notice the reaction it stirs. What is happening within your body? Is your heart racing? Can you feel your blood pressure rising? Are you sensing a fight-or-flight response to the thought?

3. Are you feeling slight or major embarrassment envisioning going back on what you once said or believed?

4. With that potential embarrassment, ask yourself, "But who cares?" Later in this book, we will get into the topic of people pleasing and how, to a fault, we care so deeply about what others think of us.

5. What resistance is now coming up for you? You are possibly wrestling God, trying to force all the pieces to match, when he continues to tell you to just quit or move on.

6. By now you are exhausted. It's like trying to push your car up an icy hill. How would it feel to raise the white flag and release this last sliver of pride you've been holding on to?

7. Ask yourself what matters most: being right and sticking to what once was or walking in God's plan for your life?

8. Now envision how it would feel to release the fears you may have around changing your mind, release your ego, not care about being right, surrender the situation, and simply allow God to open up new

doors that are beyond what you can even see or imagine. Just envision him saying to you, "_____ [name], why are you thinking so small? Do you not trust that I have greater opportunity and abundance ahead for you?"

I also want to leave you with two Scripture passages in which God explicitly asks us to let go of what once was for what's better. Isaiah 43:18–19 states, "Remember not the former things, nor consider the things of old. Behold, I am doing a new thing; now it springs forth, do you not perceive it? I will make a way in the wilderness and rivers in the desert." Here God requests that we stop looking behind us and trust in his divine plan. He will make the impossible possible. And then in Revelation 21:5, he states, "Behold, I am making all things new. . . . Write this down, for these words are trustworthy and true."

As hard as it is to release what once was or do what you swore you'd never do, there is always freedom in being able to start again or move forward. And in order to live in alignment with who you want to be and where you want to go, it's critical that you release, surrender, detach, and never say never.

Now pray this prayer with me.

Dear heavenly Father, I pray that you open my eyes to see how much you love me and how your plan is always higher than mine. Give me the strength to let go of what once was and open my hands to the infinite abundance you have waiting for me. Help me to trust like I've never trusted before. Remain heavy on my heart until I can see this different path you have for me. Give me wisdom to humbly change my mind and pivot the direction of where I once thought I was headed. Give me a glimpse of what you have possible for my life if I surrender what is good for what is excellent. Please show me how much you love me. In Jesus's name, amen.

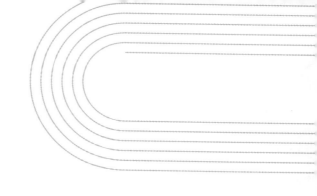

CHAPTER 2

Quit Ignoring Your Gut (And No, It's Not Your Lunch)

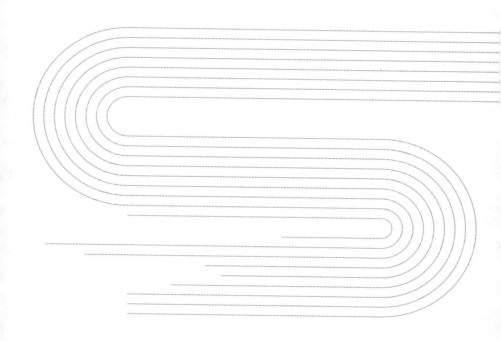

et's give them one more week and see what they offer," my then business partner suggested. At that moment, I felt it in my bones. A big, fat, *ding ding ding*, out-of-alignment moment. "Walk away before it even begins" was eating at my soul, although there was no reason for it. This collaborative deal I was working on at the start of my business career was potentially going to be my largest to date. I couldn't fathom why I felt God whispering not to do it, but rather than listen, I doubted myself. The offer that came in on the project was the kind of opportunity we might not ever get our hands on again. Well, at least at the time, that was what my emotions were telling me, which today I can clearly identify as limited thinking. And so at that moment, I completed my handy pros and cons matrix (you can find it in the *Thinking Like a Boss* book and workbook) and talked it over with my therapist, my coach, my parents, my business besties, and of course my husband and business partner. Every little bit of evidence laid out before me pointed in the direction of a yes. Everything was so intricately lined up, appearing almost too good to be true. Although my gut felt ignored, and I'm sure God did too, I just kept chalking this opportunity up to being a "God thing." There was no way he could have synchronously arranged all these little pieces for this *not* to be of him, yet I still felt uneasy. I remember the mental chatter: "Maybe I am self-sabotaging. Although I don't have a self-sabotage history. Or maybe I don't feel deserving of the amount of income this could bring in. Although I never had this big of an aversion in past business opportunities. Or maybe this potential client intimidates me because she seems so successful. Although I never really let this bother me in the past as well."

As you can see, nothing added up. The evidence to say yes to this client was apparent, the fear holding me back was practically nonexistent, and yet my gut was telling me *not* to move forward. Looking back, things should have been clear: With no valid fears present yet with such a strong reaction to stay far away, I should have gone with my gut. But going back to the consequences of ego that we discussed earlier, part of me was afraid of letting my partner down, as this was a joint deal and she felt peace over it. So I ignored my intuition— the strong nudge I was getting from God—questioned my own judgment, and stuffed my feelings down. I opened my laptop, pulled up our most recent email thread, clicked the response button, and slowly and reluctantly typed these five words: "I'm in, let's do this."

Have you ever experienced a gut-wrenching feeling in the pit of your stomach screaming at you not to do something, to stay far away, to end it now, or not to open that door? I'm sure I'm not the only one who has felt deep in their bones that something is just plain wrong. Yet, we so easily dismiss our feelings. We think, "I'd be crazy to pass up this opportunity. This is once in a lifetime. Maybe I'm overreacting. God wouldn't have brought this to me if it weren't for me. Maybe I'm trying to stay safe. Maybe I'm trying to convince myself I'm not ready. Maybe deep down I'm afraid of success or don't think I deserve happiness." The list goes on! We search for all the evidence to prove our gut feeling is wrong and have such a difficult time simply accepting that sometimes the right thing just doesn't make sense.

In this chapter, I want to have a candid conversation with you about intuition and hearing God's voice. I will be sharing some of my own experiences tuning in to and out of gut feelings and why we tend to ignore them and even blame them for something silly like indigestion at times. Anyone else? We will explore the beautiful gift God has given us as women—the gift of being so closely intertwined with our emotions. We need to embrace and tune in to our emotions and tap into the wisdom God gives us to fully receive the abundance available to us. Embracing our womanhood, tuning in to our feelings, and leaning on what we feel God is trying to communicate will invite a freedom and fullness that we've never felt before. Last, we will dive into how to get quiet and start hearing God's voice more clearly, because more likely than not, God is speaking to us all the time. Life has just been so noisy that we haven't been paying close enough attention to even notice.

Why We Ignore Our Gut

During that crazy summer of so quickly being pulled out of what I thought was right for me in my career and shoved into a full-time, stay-at-home, mamahood-homeschool stint, I started to really evaluate what I wanted as a mama. Maybe it was because I was soon to be turning thirty-five, but something in me started to question whether I was cut out for a third child. I loved our sweet little family of five (we always count Turbo, our rescue pup!), but would I have enough love and attention to possibly give one more? For a few months, I went back and forth believing I could handle a third and then deciding I was happy with two beautiful, healthy children. Until one day I was lying in bed, no phone, television, music, just silence and me. As I lay there processing my day, I felt a kick in my stomach. Now, after birthing two children, I can clearly differentiate between a gas bubble and a baby kick. This wasn't a gas bubble, and I bet you're just as confused as I was. For a split second, I put my hand on my stomach and thought, "Oh, my sweet baby just kicked," and then reality kicked me harder as I realized I maybe needed to get my mind checked because there was no baby in there. Even though it was no gas bubble, I logically thought to myself, "Indigestion—it must have been lunch" and went on with my day.

The following week as I was attempting to get Annabelle to sleep, which at the time looked like lying in her bed with her for up to an hour waiting for her to fall asleep, something else odd happened. Now, let me just preface this with my husband and I had not talked about having another baby, we had not been reading books to the girls about having babies, and don't forget we had been locked inside for months, so it wasn't like they would have heard about babies from someone else. After forty-five minutes had passed, Annabelle was asleep, and as I was attempting my escape route, I heard, "Mommy, I think we need to get Daddy a baby boy." I almost rolled right off the bed. "Annabelle, that is very sweet of you, but it takes a while for mommies and daddies to have babies, and we don't get to pick if Jesus gives us a boy or a girl." I shrugged and thought, "Oh great, where did she get this from? And even if we tried again, with my luck we would 100 percent have another girl."

Later that week, our then nineteen-month-old, who hadn't been nursed since she was ten months old, started this bizarre behavior of reaching down my shirt, grabbing my boobs, and trying to nurse what had been dried up for almost a year. I remember saying, "Baby, Mommy doesn't have milk anymore. Remember? You're a big girl now and drink from a big-girl cup." She would then scream and, when I wasn't paying attention, would pull a fast one again. The last attempt ended in a full-blown tear tantrum and was followed by something completely bizarre. If you're a mom, you'll understand, and for the rest of you, well, we learn something new every day! The nontechnical term is the screaming baby letdown—when nursing moms experience an automatic milk flow when *any* baby cries. However, this typically happens early on in the breastfeeding journey and tends to fade in time. Well, I felt it and looked down, and both girls shouted, "Milk!" At least this confirmed I wasn't delusional. However, maybe this meant I was pregnant. No, there was no way it could be possible based on where I was in my cycle, which I had religiously tracked for years. "I must just be reading into something that's not there. All these instances must just be a coincidence. Here I go again reading into things because of my silly gut feelings. I'll just take a pregnancy test to prove I must be wrong." Have you ever felt this way? Maybe in your career or personal life, you feel these internal tugs, yet you fight them and even at times work against this beautiful innate gift of intuition available to you.

Now, I highly doubt that I get more of these heavenly bread crumbs than anyone else. But what I do know for certain is that I've become really good at paying attention and not ignoring them throughout the years. As far back as middle school, I can remember having gut feelings and even dreams that I would ignore because "that would be weird," and then later I would watch the situations play out. Like the time I dreamed my then boyfriend dumped me at the fifth-grade Christmas pageant to ask out (whatever that meant back then) my best friend. Which ended up playing out exactly as I remembered it from my dream but with 1990s blue mascara dripping down my face in the real version. I have always had this internal struggle with gut feelings—partially believing and partially doubting and denying. And this would happen over and over with small and big things. Has the same been true for you? Can you think of any past examples off the top of your head? If so, jot them down in the margins before you forget—they will be helpful later in this chapter.

Why do so many of us ignore these divine downloads when we ultimately know that they often end up being spot-on? It all comes down to trust—self-trust and our trust in God. We have a really hard time believing anything that we can't see or conceptualize. Yes, we believe in God and the miracles he performs, but if one of those miracles were to happen to us, our natural inclination might be to see it as luck. We read about people being prophetic in Bible times, but today when someone admits hearing from God, many automatically jump to "Oh, honey, maybe you should get some rest; you've been working so hard." It comes down to not accepting or admitting because we don't want to appear weird or off our rockers, or we don't want to offend others because deep down we are innate people pleasers, which we will get more into further along in the book. I truly believe that sensing God's voice, gut feelings, intuition, divine downloads, or whatever you want to call them are a beautiful gift that is available to each of us today. However, because of our innate desire for people to like us, we don't allow ourselves to tap into this beautiful relationship of self-trust and trust in God. Because of how we are conditioned to think in society, through scary movies and television shows that mock Christianity (think of the typical fortune-teller or "God told me to do it" scene), we tend to disconnect ourselves from our gut feelings, either thinking that "hearing voices is crazy" or feeling shame that we are doing something wrong like tapping into something not of God. It is important to acknowledge that God does speak to us, whether through signs or through others, and this is clearly discussed in the Bible. Here are two verses that have always stood out to me in which a message was given not once but twice in the Bible regarding hearing God's voice.

> And it shall come to pass afterward,
> that I will pour out my Spirit on all flesh;
> your sons and your daughters shall prophesy,
> your old men shall dream dreams,
> and your young men shall see visions. (Joel 2:28)

And in the last days it shall be, God declares, that I will pour out my Spirit on all flesh, and your sons and your daughters shall prophesy, and your young men shall see visions, and your old men shall dream dreams. (Acts 2:17)

Interestingly, if we search the Bible for the most common words we use for prophecy today, such as *intuition* or *gut feelings*, we won't find a thing about them in the Bible. I believe that because of this, many are afraid to tap into this special gift. But if we search for *prophecy*, we will find dozens of verses that talk about it.

How often do you question the feelings on your heart? I'm sure if you took some time today, you would be able to look back and recall past situations when you ignored your gut and wish you had trusted yourself and done the opposite. I bet you felt that tug of your soul literally begging you to trust, listen, and not care about what others will think, but you held back in fear of appearing nuts, people judging you, or even judging yourself. When we can acknowledge that we let ourselves down in the past and line the evidence up, we can then one by one use these examples as evidence for our future decisions. These past experiences are what provide the future evidence for us to release all judgment, follow our feelings, and realize what a beautiful gift they are. And by doing this, we can begin experiencing life to its fullest. Following our intuition and hearing God's voice will enable us to live a life of complete alignment—peace, trust, and freedom from judgment. It truly is a supernatural place to be. And guess what? It's available to each and every one of us!

Our Innate Female Connection

As humans, we are always searching for evidence to prove that we are either right or wrong. Even when discussing this concept with you, it pains me that I can't get my hands on quantifiable evidence *proving* that women have an innate gift of feeling and understanding. But the qualitative stories that we bear witness to do imply it. As I am writing this in the midst of the Christmas season, I think of Mary and how God chose a young virgin to birth Jesus and deliver the message of his purpose into the world. Can you just imagine trying to explain to people that you were a virgin pregnant with the Messiah? I mean, I think back to the times I felt I was losing my marbles over little signs or feelings, but poor Mary! She must have literally felt like she was losing it. And to top it all off, what were her friends and family thinking?

But you see, God knew that she was strong and capable and had enough self-trust to be the one to carry out this mission. I believe that God chose women to be the ones to grow and birth babies because it takes a high level of mental strength to endure the ups and downs of pregnancy, including the emotional strength needed to physically push a human out of you. Whether you have, want to have, don't want to have, are having trouble conceiving, or are undecided whether you will have children, just know that as a woman, babies or not, you have an emotional strength and resilience that you can't even fathom. Take a moment to let that sink in. Maybe even highlight it so you can come back to it at a time when you are questioning your strength. You have more resilience than you will ever need to tap into.

Now, back to the Mary story. I'm not sure if you are aware, but what I find fascinating is that before the angel Gabriel appeared to Mary to tell her she would give birth to not only a baby boy but also the Son of God, the Messiah, he appeared to Zechariah, the husband of Mary's cousin Elizabeth. Gabriel told Zechariah that Elizabeth would also be having a son, John. But because they had been unable to conceive, Zechariah did not believe the angel and reacted much differently than Mary did. Let's just say he was spooked. Because of Zechariah's skepticism, the angel decided to silence him, leaving him completely mute until Elizabeth gave birth many months later. Can you imagine if each time we doubted our gut feelings or what God was impressing on our hearts, we became silenced until it came to pass? This is a powerful lesson for us not to be ashamed but to be emboldened to share when we feel something on our hearts.

We need to acknowledge that we have this God-given gift. It's important that we embrace our emotions and the intuitive wisdom God has placed within us. When we can tune in to and rely on what we feel God is trying to communicate to us, we can experience a freedom, fullness, and abundance that we never imagined could be available for us. When I learned to quit ignoring my feelings, I noticed something really interesting—life began feeling easier. I began to see how for many years I had been in an ongoing internal battle with my feelings. Rather than believing them, I was pushing against them and stuffing down what I knew so deeply to be true. And although I still doubt my gut at times, let's just say I've come a long way. In the day-to-day instances, I now can stop, listen, and honor these feelings.

Going back to that opening story, the early business deal—well, let's just say that ignoring God's prompting didn't work out so well for me. It ended up being an incredible learning experience, but a painful one. Very soon into the business relationship, I could see why God had placed that restlessness within me—to protect me from some unfortunate disappointments that were about to happen. And about a year after the situation ended, I really felt him impressing these words on my heart: "Kate, I was trying to protect you all along, but your logical human mind clouded your decision-making. Rather than thinking more abundantly, you accepted something that at the time seemed of significant value, when I had even more that was easily available for you. I tried showing you to protect you from the pain you had to experience that year." What I painfully learned is that God doesn't choose for us to experience pain or loss. At times, he might even give us the wisdom to shelter us from it.

Trust me, friend, we have *all* been there—what we see as clear evidence and facts isn't always accurate. But what is accurate is the voice of God. It's not easy to discern what God is trying to tell us, which is why it's so important that we get quiet and practice listening for his voice in the small things so that we are ready for the big things.

Now, I'm sure you're wondering what happened with the baby story. I won't go into all the crazy things that happened leading up to the pregnancy test, but let's just say that over the next week I completely tore the house apart and cleaned and rearranged all the furniture. My husband (having no idea what had been happening to me) casually and jokingly asked if I was nesting. Then the day after the milk incident I had my yearly OB-GYN exam (that had been planned out months prior), where I was asked if I was ready for a third baby and told that if I was, I should consider having one sooner rather than later due to my age. I uncomfortably replied with, "We are in no rush; we will just let God decide for us."

For some odd reason, they didn't do a pregnancy test at the doctor's office that day, but I had a sneaking suspicion, putting all the pieces together the following day, that maybe God was just trying to shout in my face that I actually was qualified and capable to be a mama to a third child. But again, there was a zero percent chance I could be pregnant according to my monthly tracking app. And when I say impossible, let's just say weeks later when I went for the ultrasound and handed the doctor this "impossible" date of conception, he replied with, "Yeah, with your cycle, there is no way that a baby could be made on that date. I know how easy it can be to confuse dates; your baby has to be nine weeks old. Lie down, let's take a look." Sidenote for anyone else who has ever experienced a male OB-GYN. Why is it that it's always so easy for women to confuse dates? When I last checked, don't men typically rely on women to remind them of dates and keep them on schedule? At least that's been my experience! Anyway, as he was looking at the baby wiggling around on the screen and I was internally rolling my eyes at him, he appeared rather flabbergasted. "Is something wrong?" I asked, as I knew what his answer was going to be. "Um, no, nothing is wrong, but this is an almost twelve-week baby, which makes no sense at all. This baby clearly is fully developed. I don't understand how this could be possible. There was a zero percent chance you could have gotten pregnant when you did." Yep, there was also a zero percent chance many miracles Jesus performed could happen, but when he has a plan, there is no getting in his way.

I'm not exactly sure why this happened to me, but what I do know is that when God has a message to share with us, nothing will hold him back from getting our attention. He has impeccable timing and quite a sense of humor, and in this instance, he dropped many little seeds over that few-week period of time to get me thinking more about mamahood. And because I wasn't yet convinced I'd be qualified to have a third child, he took matters into his own hands and gave us a child when there was a zero percent chance we would get pregnant. And just like Annabelle mumbled in her sleep that night, it did end up being a baby boy for Daddy. How cool is it that God can use children to deliver messages to us? And how neat is it that hearing his voice can begin even before we have any insight into it? Maybe that's the beauty in listening to the Holy Spirit—listening with a childlike innocence.

So if you want your life to feel more filled with ease and less resistance, then let down your guard and start accepting what you hear God telling you. Being able to lead with gut feelings and be confident in your decisions will save you a ton of time and, bottom line, heartache. I can't tell you how many times I've heard women say to me, "I just wish I had listened to my gut. I knew it all along. God was clearly trying to protect me, but my thinking was clouded by the opportunity or the dollar signs or the desire to be loved." Time and time again, I've witnessed this as a therapist with clients discussing dating or marital relationships, motherhood, or careers, and also with my business coaching clients regarding business deals and relationships. It can be gut-wrenching when we go against what we know deep down to be true.

However, what a beautiful thing to witness when women *do* lean in and listen to what God is nudging them with. Below are a few words I have had the honor to hear:

- "Because I walked away from a relationship that didn't feel right or God honoring, I met my now husband."
- "Because I said no to a job offer that could have paid the bills but I could sense wasn't quite aligned, I was a day later offered the job I had been waiting years for."

- "Because I casually dropped by my daughter's house to say hi, I was able to help her when her dog jumped over the fence and ran away."

What I would love to have you do now is take a moment to jot down big and small times that you did listen to that inner prompting. I want you to have these examples readily available because often when we are in the moment of decision-making, we can easily forget past experiences. If you haven't had the chance to listen to an inner nudge, not to worry. I will walk you through how to become more aware, as you probably have had many divine downloads but just haven't noticed or put the pieces together just yet.

Getting in Tune with Your Heart

So now for the best part: How can we get our hearts in line and beating with God's voice? Well, here is the good news—it's a lot easier than you think. You are already fully capable of doing this! We were freely given the tools and ability to tap into and listen to God's promptings. It just takes a little work and intention, friend. And then of course the bad news—often, *easy* for us complicated humans ends up not always being so easy. We allow emotions such as doubt or the desire to be liked by others to suffocate and hold us captive. We often feel more comfortable living out of alignment, with patterns or behaviors that are not serving us, than stepping out of our comfort zone and shifting our behaviors to place us in alignment. Hearing God's voice and better translating what we feel he is impressing on our hearts requires really just four things: belief, willingness, quieting the noise, and active listening.

First, we have to believe that God does indeed speak to us, dropping divine downloads we can decode or tap into so we can make more aligned choices in life. First Corinthians 14:1 says, "Pursue love, and earnestly desire the spiritual gifts, especially that you may prophesy." Once we believe that God's Word is alive and true and that he is still working through us, we can begin to receive this gift.

Second, we must have a willing heart—willing to do what might feel out of our comfort zones, willing to potentially appear awkward, and willing to possibly be rejected by those we love. Even Jesus was rejected on earth—people mocked him for saying he was the Son of God. And even after he rose on the third day, some still did not believe it. Think of all those who have gone before us who were willing to appear a little strange for a good cause. How willing are you to do what might feel uncomfortable to begin walking in peace, freedom, and abundance?

Third, we need to learn to quiet the noise, slow down the speed, invite margin into our lives, and find stillness. Ask yourself these three questions:

1. How can I clear the mental clutter so that I have more space to think and allow God to speak into my heart?
2. How can I release what is no longer serving me so that I have margin and flexibility to process what he is placing on my heart?
3. How can I begin saying no to mediocre opportunities to open up space to be present for what means the most to me?

When our lives are filled to the brim, it's very hard for God's words to come through to us. Have you ever really wanted to share something with a friend who you sensed was too busy to talk? Maybe it's been vice versa and someone has said, "Oh, you seem busy; let me try to catch you at a better time." Imagine that friend being God, trying to send us a message that we have little space to receive. This is why we need to always keep space for the wonder of life to fit in.

Fourth, we need to learn to listen. How often are we really listening? I think it's hard to listen when we have music, podcasts, television, and movies all playing in the background. How often do you drive your car or go for a walk in complete silence? There certainly is a time and a place for multitasking; however, we also need to make space so it is easy to listen as well. A good way to practice intentional listening with God is to start being a better listener to those around you, to be fully intentional when people are speaking to you, even taking paper or mental notes.

Ever watch a movie or listen to a song a few times and notice something different? It's the same when listening to God's promptings. We may hear him impress something on our hearts once, but we need to hear again and again to really uncover what he is trying to tell us. I find that God loves revealing himself through dreams, and I believe it's because it's a time we are still and only able to listen and receive. Just this week I had a vivid dream about a friend's childhood that I felt God was impressing on me to share with her. When I woke up, I decided to take some notes so I wouldn't miss a thing. I recorded exactly what I saw, felt, and experienced and what I felt it might mean for her, and I sent her the recording. If I had just gone on with my day and not been actively listening by engaging in what I was hearing, I most likely would have forgotten some of the important pieces. She was so grateful I did this, as it confirmed a lot of what she had been working on confidentially with her therapist for many years, which gave her a great sense of peace and answers to some questions.

Summing It All Up

Now I want to give you one last piece of advice as we close this chapter: Be patient with yourself. Learning to trust and understand your intuition or what you feel God is telling you takes time, often takes missing it, and takes a whole lot of trial and error. And the only way to get better at it is through experience. I'd love to encourage you today to consider starting a journal or a note on your phone where you can begin collecting these divine downloads, God winks, or little signs or feelings you experience. Write down the date next to them and include some context. This will set you up for better trusting your gut feelings and following them more easily when they occur because you will start to see connections. Often it is the obscure words that someone might say to you or you might notice that in time give you the largest confirmation of what God wants to tell you.

One thing that brought me complete peace about even attempting a writing career after failing out of my English literature minor was having someone with whom I had a falling out several years prior contact me and tell me that they had a vision of my face on the front and back of a book. I hadn't spoken to this man in years, and I can't imagine the level of risk and unease he probably felt reaching out to share these words, but he said he could not hold back. And this brought me to tears, as I had not yet shared with a single soul that I had started pursuing this dream. When you can risk feeling a little crazy, listen more to what God is trying to tell you, and follow his lead, I can assure you that life will begin to feel not only aligned but also in line with his greater purpose for you.

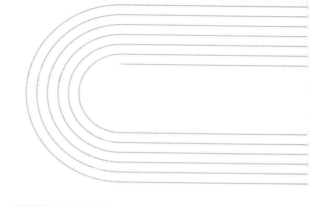

CHAPTER 3

Bye-Bye, People Pleasing

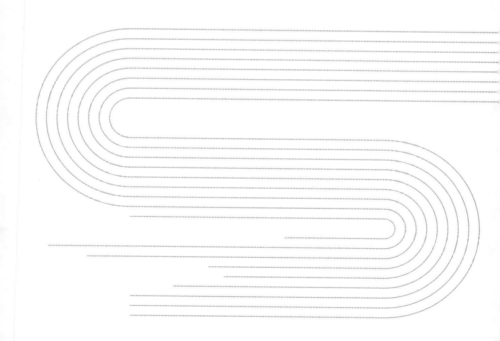

As I sit here and close my eyes, earnestly trying to think back to where it all started, it feels like a distant dream a lifetime ago that I don't want to remember. In the winter of 2009, I was in my second semester at Columbia University getting my master's degree. I had gone away for college but had always had roommates and lived out of suitcases. This was the first time having my very own studio apartment with real furniture and a yearlong lease, which allowed me to actually leave my belongings put during holidays when I would go visit family. This should have been the best time of my life, but as you'll see, I was learning something very new to me that in my twenty-two years of life I never knew was available: boundaries. I had been a perpetual, perfectionistic people pleaser my entire life, always wanting people to like me, only showing my best self—pretending to have it all together and never revealing even a droplet of vulnerability. To everyone around me, I just smiled and claimed everything was great. Life was great. School was great. The only people who saw the other side were my parents, not even my best friends.

However, I was slowly dying inside and out. I was emotionally and physically exhausted chasing perfectionistic goals that I never felt I could grasp. As I talked about in my first book, a little over two months prior to this, I had my first breakdown. I cried to my boyfriend and a close friend and told them who the real me really was—an insecure people pleaser who would do anything to get ahead, who hated herself, her body, and who she was becoming. They knew something was off and encouraged me to get help. For the first time in my life, I stepped foot into therapy and got my first diagnosis handed to me on a slip of paper, along with a bottle of pills and this statement from my therapist: "If you had continued down this path, Kate, you would have ended up in a hospital. You had nothing left to you; you were slowly killing yourself." Wow. I sort of had an idea how bad the eating disorder was, but I also just thought I wanted to be pretty, have people like me, and look cute in my outfits like all the cool girls in *Us Weekly* magazine. Although everyone thought I had it together—good grades, Ivy League school, beautiful Upper West Side apartment, stylish clothes, a boyfriend, more friends than I could handle—she was right. I was slowly killing myself. I had never felt this lonely before.

When I would want to avoid my feelings or escape the unrealistic high standards I had set for my life, I would walk from 71st and Broadway down to the Lincoln Center Barnes & Noble. It was exactly a one-mile round-trip walk, which meant it would cancel out the calories of a chai tea with skim and a drop of honey or a coffee with a splash of soy. It was my safe place. I would walk through the revolving doors and head straight to the escalators, hop right on, and take in all the books while riding to the third-floor café and magazine area. I would then grab all the magazines that had skinny girls on the covers, carry my stack to the café, order my warm drink, park at a table, and sit there for hours, looking at how perfect their lives were and envisioning how I could make mine that way too.

"What can I do to make people like me better? Maybe if I just lose another five pounds I will seem more confident and put-together? I wonder what new outfits I can get to make me appear older and be more respected at my internship? Maybe I should start wearing heels more often—that might work. Boy, am I hungry right now. Those Rice Krispies treats look amazing. No, I can't get one. People probably already think I look like a fat slob, and I'm going for more dignified and ladylike, so I'll eat a carrot when I get home."

If you know me today, you won't even recognize anything I am saying. I actually question whether you will believe me because of the stark difference between my life today and my life fourteen years ago. You probably wonder how it could even be possible to go from such distorted, obsessive thinking to living a life quite the opposite. Well, let's just say this: It is possible. So many of you can probably relate in some sense with the desire to be seen and liked by those around you. You may not be going to as extreme measures as I was, but you are slowly suffocating yourself, swimming to the surface but never quite coming up for air. Before we go any further, let me just share this with you: Life is absolutely not supposed to be this way. Living life to please others is not God's will for us, never has been, and never will be. God's design for your life is to live in community with others, not to feel solely responsible for pleasing the entire community. Even Jesus couldn't please everyone during his time here on earth, right? That was exactly why he chose the Twelve, to pour into them and to entrust them to stretch their resources and then pour into others. He was really good at setting boundaries, a master at setting limits, asking for what he needed, and being unapologetic when saying no to protect his energy. So why do we have so much trouble doing the same?

In this chapter, we are going to identify what people pleasing looks like, uncover where this desire to be liked comes from, how it serves us but also enslaves us, and how to release ourselves from it so that we can live the lives God designed for us to live, free from people pleasing and in alignment with his purpose and calling for our lives. Even if you don't consider yourself a people pleaser, please still read this chapter because somewhere deep down we all have a desire to be liked. I know that personally I have come an almost unrecognizably long way; however, if I am not mindful by checking in with my heart often, I can easily slip back into old patterns. So, friend, let's dive in!

Is This You?

Life feels exhausting. You are constantly striving to make everyone happy. Do any of these describe you?

- You say yes to extra projects at work, stay late, and sometimes take work home with you on the weekends. You think to yourself, "Maybe she will notice how invested I am in the company and promote me."
- You volunteer every Sunday in the nursery, lead Bible study, and are involved in the inner-city soup kitchen ministry. Church used to fill you up, but now you walk away each week feeling depleted and pressured to say yes to one more thing. You constantly hear,

"We just don't know how you can handle it all! You are superwoman. We are so lucky to have someone like you in our church."

• You are juggling your business, are in charge of the school PTA, have one potty training and one in diapers nursing, and the only time you have to do your work for your master's degree is 4 to 6 a.m. before the kids wake up, breakfast is served, and you need to run them to school or day care while your husband is at spin class. He says, "I just don't know how you do it all" and even brought you flowers today with a card you have yet to open because your hands are busy folding the third load of laundry while dinner is simmering on the stovetop.

Woo-hoo! Congratulations, friend! You have officially earned your certificate of living your life for everyone else but yourself. You are chugging cups of coffee and spending way too much money on makeup to cover up those bags under your eyes. Or maybe you've decided to wear glasses so no one can really notice the exhaustion in your face—I mean, who has time for makeup these days when we are all out there trying to save the world? Now, please do me a favor and lean in. I have three important questions for you today.

1. Are you really happy?
2. Is this really how you want to live your life?
3. Does it feel good hearing, "You are superwoman; never change" or "I don't know how you do it all, but keep doing it"?

Okay, I'm just going to keep it real with you because I'm about 95 percent certain no one else in your life will because they like how perfect you serves them. Here's the reality: When I see you, I really see you. And you are hollow. You have nothing left to give. You are beyond exhausted, running on fumes and coffee, scrambling to keep up just to win the next gold star, and this is hands down *not* God's plan for your life, sister. You were made to live a life of peace, joy, and abundance and to actually experience those feelings yourself, not just give them all away. I love how John 10:10 so simply depicts this: "The thief comes only to steal and kill and destroy; I have come that they may have life, and have it to the full" (NIV). Jesus came so that we would have the privilege of living life to the full, not a life filled with never-ending tasks.

Where People Pleasing Begins, How It Serves Us, How It Enslaves Us

Let's start with Proverbs 29:25: "Fearing people is a dangerous trap, but trusting the LORD means safety" (NLT). You may not even be aware that people pleasing is a part of your life. This might be so deeply ingrained in you that you have no insight whatsoever that this is actually not normal. I hate using the word *normal*, because, I mean, what really is normal? But just know that on a spectrum, living solely to please others is the complete opposite of living a life completely for yourself, only taking and never giving. And God has not intended for us to live life either of those ways. We are called to find a balance somewhere in the middle, respecting our own needs, limits, and desires while still loving others around us well.

So where does people pleasing start? If you had asked me five years ago before I became a mother, I probably would have said middle-school age, when kids' minds are so fixated on belonging. "I'll be your best friend if you don't tell the teacher." "I'll invite you to my birthday party if you let me borrow five dollars." "I won't tell Johnny you wear deodorant if you let me sit next to him at lunch." Kids are cruel! However, today, after having littles myself, I can see that the desire to be liked begins at an even younger age. I've witnessed my daughters, as young as two, vying for our attention and to be acknowledged. While writing this, we are in full-blown two- and three-year-old land. I never envisioned humans this young being this competitive and grappling for a parent's attention at the expense of another. Guys, it's brutal! "Mommy, you should put Chawlieee to bed because she isn't listening. But I'm listening and picked up my toys, so I get to sit with you to watch *Moana*." The desire to be noticed, to be liked, to be acknowledged is something innate in us. And because of how we grow up, are raised, or raise our children, we reinforce this notion of "Let's make Mommy and Daddy happy." This then translates later into making teachers and peers happy, and then eventually it's just a part of us that we have adapted into adulthood within our careers and relationships.

So why do we keep it going? Why do we perpetually people please when maybe we have an inkling that it's not the healthiest thing? We do it because it serves a purpose for us—in many ways, it makes us feel good. We are being acknowledged. People are noticing us and making us feel seen, desired, appreciated, sometimes solely from acknowledgment. So what we receive from it and what serves us—being seen—is a vicious cycle, because it's also the exact thing that is hurting us. We thrive on positive reinforcement. When someone thanks us, whether it's sincere or not, it signals something to our brains that gives us an instant boost of dopamine. And when we receive this acknowledgment, it motivates us to want to receive it more, because it feels really good! And even if we know that the pattern or behavior isn't the healthiest, it enslaves us and feels virtually impossible to quit because each time our brains are being rewarded.

I think of the example of the cycle of violence, which I have always viewed as a behavior pattern for any type of manipulator, not exclusive to a person of violence. I am going to use the example of those in an abusive intimate relationship. The man is charming with words, tells the woman he loves and cares about her, and wins her over. Little by little, she begins to see his true colors. He is irritable, no longer as patient, talks over her, doesn't let her have a say in anything, and no longer shows any effort to praise her like he did in the beginning. He is plain distant. So what does she do? She tries harder. She does everything she can to get him to adjust his mood and go back to that place of praising her. And then what typically happens is the breaking point, where he can't take the smothering or niceness anymore, snaps, says mean things, maybe even has a violent outburst. She feels hurt and sad, usually not angry at first, blames herself, and desires for things to go back to where they were in the beginning. Then he potentially feels remorse or manipulates the remorse by pulling at her heart strings and apologizes so she doesn't leave. Then he is back at stage one of the cycle, using words and actions to win her over. For many cycles or indefinitely, she accepts his words and actions because they are worth that hit of dopamine.

This is obviously an extreme example, but perhaps you can see that you either are in some sort of arrangement right now or were in the past that you stayed in because, although it wasn't ideal, ultimately, you ended up being seen, feeling acknowledged, or not being rejected. I can remember being in a pretty crappy relationship in my younger years, and because my self-esteem was nonexistent and my people pleasing tendencies were at an all-time high, I continued to date this person because maybe once a week he told me I was pretty and I so deeply wanted to be noticed and seen. Looking back now as a fierce woman with an incredible husband who loves and respects me, I am working hard, along with my husband, to change this narrative for our little girls (and son), teaching them that "pretty" doesn't mean anything. They are so much more than how they look, and their confidence should never depend on how others view their outward appearance. How does this translate for you today?

Something I always suggest to clients is to start new relationships from the place you want your relationships to be in the future. If you are bad at establishing boundaries right now, start relationships with much clearer limits. Or if you already have really firm boundaries with your close family and friends, start new relationships from this same place. What I often see with clients is actually quite the opposite. Many show up to new relationships wanting to be liked, so they offer a perfect version of themselves, which is virtually impossible to maintain. And in many ways, I get it—we want to gain people's admiration and trust. Often we idolize people we admire, look up to, want to be connected to. So the best way to begin any new relationship is to keep the long term at the forefront of your mind. Set limits early, earn respect, and do not set yourself up to have to go back and change. If people don't like you early on with the limits you have set, there is no way they will like you if you're a pushover at the beginning and then all of a sudden set boundaries.

I can't tell you how many times in my career I've come close to overstepping my own boundaries in situations of wanting to be liked by someone new. The problem is typically with maintaining firm boundaries with work hours. I'm often tempted to let them slide for someone new I'd like to collaborate with. However, it turns out that often people will understand when you tell them your work hours and will respect why you can't go beyond them. And by setting limits, you're also modeling positive behavior for them to follow and apply in their own life if they aren't already. I often hear, "Wow, I really admire that you can stick to a schedule. I wish I could cut back my business hours as well." I then share my secret—sticking to my own boundaries and releasing the need to please and accommodate everyone else's schedule. And, my friends, this will set a precedent and unshakable foundation for healthy relationships.

Setting limits even before a relationship starts can save you a ton of time, heartache, and frustration down the road. Quick example. When I opened my first business, a psychotherapy practice, I decided to have each new client sign a ten-page office policies packet that included what-to-do-if scenarios: What if we bumped into each other at a restaurant, one of us had a fever, it snowed, they needed a court letter written, one of us was running late, etc. Essentially, any scenario you could think of that could potentially come up during the lifetime of their treatment. My colleagues thought I was crazy, told me no one would sign it, and that it would most likely turn people away and ruin the relationship before it even started. Fast-forward several years into private practice, and it actually did exactly what I had hoped it would do: It made the therapeutic alliance smoother. Clients reported referring to the manual, finding an answer easily spelled out rather than needing to worry, ruminate, or ask about potential scenarios. And my colleagues? They complained about their clients not having boundaries, texting them on weekends, showing up with the flu, and friending them on social media. So, do you see how not worrying about how others perceive you early on can actually strengthen a relationship and save you time and a headache?

No matter how much we want to deny it, we all innately desire to be liked, understood, and seen. Where would you say that desire is most present for you today? Do you desire to be acknowledged by your boss for all those after-hours you've been spending on that project? Do you desire to hear from family, friends, or your partner how they don't quite know how you do it all? Please know that although people pleasing has served you by giving you a sense of belonging or not rocking the boat, there are so many more benefits to having boundaries—the potential for peace, joy, and fulfillment and the opportunity to feel respected. I know it's never fun to need to lay down the law early on in a relationship or to rock the boat in an existing one, but the sooner you become okay with not needing to please everyone and being willing to change, the sooner you can begin embracing the freedom God has ready and available for you.

Do You Know What You Want?

Now I'm curious, friend. What do you really want for your life? I bet in many ways you feel put on the spot being asked this right now. You have lived to serve and please others for so long that the vision for your future dreams and desires may appear covered in cobwebs, a distant memory that you aren't even quite sure is in alignment anymore. Although you feel like an about-to-crack hollow chocolate Easter bunny, you also feel safe. People around you like what you do for them. Life is exhausting, but it feels good to be acknowledged even for just the small things. It feels too risky to let this all go and start working on your own dreams.

You may think to yourself,

- "If I stop this now, I will lose everything."
- "My friends are used to me being the one who drops everything for them."
- "My boss will promote someone else if I stop staying late and working weekends."
- "I'll no longer be called superwoman by my church community if I only serve in the nursery."
- "My marriage has always been this way with me doing it all. I have no idea how my husband will react if I go on strike and begin asking him to help."

Do any of these scenarios ring true for you today? Are you afraid to set limits for fear of being rejected, rocking the boat, or upsetting others? Well, here's the lowdown. When you set limits with others, three very important things happen.

First, you are standing your ground, honoring your own needs and desires, and respecting yourself. You are saying, "I am worth it. I trust that I am so in alignment with my intuition and God's purpose for me that I have no other choice but to respect my limits and not overstep them."

Second, when you set limits and follow through with not giving in, in time, others will follow your lead. Yes, there might be some friction at first and hard conversations, but they will begin to respect this newer, more confident version of you.

And last, if they don't respect you, you are in a great place! This means this person has been around only for their own personal gain. They are not willing to engage in a healthy give-and-take relationship, and their walking away opens up more time and more space for you to welcome in new people who will respect your boundaries.

Now when I suggest that clients, friends, family, and acquaintances in my life begin taking inventory as to why they are constantly striving to please others and reconsider these behaviors, I almost immediately sense panic in their voices. "Oh, my goodness, I can't do that. So-and-so will lose it. I've been playing this role with them forever. New relationships, maybe, but I can't change things with these people right now." Does this fear come up for you too? Fear of losing what you so desire to hear or receive—being needed and being seen? I know that at this place you are in today, it doesn't feel easy to consider letting this old behavior go, but the only way to live a life of more peace, less burnout, and more intentionality is to release your old ways of thinking and doing. To step into true alignment and God's full and abundant purpose and calling for our lives, we need to release ourselves from our innate people pleasing tendencies.

The How

This is the most exciting part of this chapter—seeing how we can change our people pleasing habits. For some reason, when we fear change, we make the situation out to be a lot bigger in our minds than it really is. We play out elaborate stories of what might possibly happen. And then here is what typically happens: Rather than putting one foot in front of the other and stepping into possibility, we sit in indecision, allow time to pass, and develop even more hypothetical situations in our minds. And what was once a slight possibility—"They will reject me"—becomes an absolute done deal in our minds. So let's get this clear. Here is what I am *not* asking for. I am not asking for you to set up walls around you so that you begin refusing new relationships or stop engaging in your current ones. What I am asking for is a willingness to begin in the small places. Releasing people pleasing tendencies doesn't happen overnight and could possibly be a lifelong process. As I mentioned earlier, although I semi-recovered from people pleasing many years ago, this doesn't mean I don't have to work on my behavior even today. In times of extreme stress, striving can become my default, providing safety and control. "If I do for others and go above and beyond, I will receive praise." See what I mean? I have to continually check in with myself to ensure I do not fall back into my past behaviors.

The following guidelines will help you release the desire to please and step into the true desires of your heart:

1. Be flexible with yourself. Going back to chapter 1, it's important that you do not create absolutes but allow

what feels right or what doesn't feel right to shift with your environment, life season, and so on. Setting overarching rules for yourself or others can lead to very rigid tendencies, leaving you feeling stuck, others feeling pushed away, and ultimately you feeling even more out of alignment than before. A mantra I encourage you to recite throughout this process is "What feels good for me right now is allowed to shift at any time. There are no set rules, and I can make them up as I go. I am allowed to change my mind at any time." The key here is flexibility, grace, and compassion with yourself. This isn't easy. However, by releasing the need to be liked, you will find that life will become easier.

2. Take inventory of where people pleasing is most prevalent for you. Does the behavior appear in all the relationships in your life or just at work or with friends? Are there people you are not afraid to lay down the law with, or are you allowing everyone in your life to take advantage of you? I see people pleasing tendencies come up more often with those who are farthest from the home, meaning people are more willing to go to extremes with those they are the least close to in order to impress them. It often feels safer to let your partner down than your new boss or new BFF on Instagram. We often take drastic measures to win these people over, which then sets us up for failure.

3. Remind yourself that it's okay to question or request clarification about something. So often when wanting to impress, we quickly say yes to something we

know very little about. For instance, we may feel guilty asking for a contract in a work relationship. This happened to me not too long ago with a man I highly respected in my industry. I felt like a nuisance asking almost half a dozen times for a contract, but I knew in the long run that setting this limit early would set a precedent that "this girl don't play in business!" Once we began working together, I then needed to be firm when negotiating a joint business deal. Again, I felt like the bad guy at several points, but I know how much he actually appreciated my assertiveness and ability to clearly ask for what I needed. So I repeat, *never* feel bad about asking questions or establishing ground rules. Doing so will save you from a headache or possible confrontation down the road.

4. Allow resistance to come up for you. You are going to experience push and pull, especially when first attempting to stop people pleasing. You might coach yourself to set boundaries but then ten minutes later chicken out. My friend, this is normal. New behaviors are going to feel awkward because they're new, but eventually putting your needs first will become a habit, which will make doing it easier. What can help when experiencing this resistance is envisioning how good you will feel when you follow through with your plan. Think of the confidence you will be cultivating and how each and every time you push through this resistance it will begin to feel just a little easier, until someday it will be second nature.

5. Get comfortable sitting with the possibility of someone being upset with you. You have to stand firm in your belief. Speak up for what you want and do what you know is right for you. As resistance surfaces for you, know that it is bound to come up for others as well when you are laying down new laws. The natural response will be to apologize and people please even more, but you have to resist the urge to do so and sit in the uncomfortableness. So what if they don't like you speaking up? What gives them the right to choose how you live your life? The main thing here is not to be shaken. So often when I'm working with clients, resistance will come up when I point something out to them. They often get frustrated, become angry with me, and are even rude. However, once they see I am not shaken by their behavior and I stick to what I've pointed out, their demeanor changes. I give them the space to state their frustrations—they are entitled to that—but in a way that doesn't diminish what I said. When I stand firm, a powerful healing environment is created that many clients have never experienced before. And this is where major breakthrough occurs for them, as no one in their lives has ever stood that firm and spoken that much truth to them.

6. Give yourself buckets of grace when you fall. Notice I said "when"? That's because people pleasing is bound to resurface in some big or small way in the future for each of us. When I was launching my book, it hadn't even occurred to me that my people pleasing tendencies could reappear. I thought for sure they were behind me. I felt blindsided. When

everything is stripped away, our eyes are opened to the realities of life, 20/20 vision is restored, and we begin to see cracks and remnants of where we unknowingly pushed our own limits in hopes of pleasing others. And the only way to move forward is to give ourselves a great big hug and a warm blanket of grace.

I want you to take this verse, meditate on it, write it down on Post-it Notes, stick them all over your home, and continue each and every day to hold it closely to your heart: "For we speak as messengers approved by God to be entrusted with the Good News. Our purpose is to please God, not people. He alone examines the motives of our hearts" (1 Thess. 2:4 NLT). Each and every time you are tempted to slip into your old ways of overstepping your own boundaries to gain people's respect, use this verse to help you remember that your life's purpose is not to please people but to please God. Period.

- When you feel people are trying to sway you to believe in something that doesn't sit right with you, ask yourself, "Is this pleasing to God? Or am I trying to bow to man?"
- When you fear saying no at your job when your boss asks you to fudge some numbers, ask yourself, "Is this pleasing to God? Or am I trying to please man?"
- When your moms group starts bad-mouthing the mom who didn't make it that day, ask yourself, "Is this pleasing to God? Or am I not speaking up in fear of them judging me?"

We are bound to find ourselves in similar situations each and every day the rest of our lives, and how we decide to approach them will determine the kind of lives we will live. Are we living to please others or living with clear boundaries that will lead us to a life of peace, joy, fulfillment, and abundance?

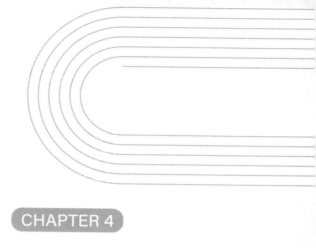

CHAPTER 4

Stop the Worry Cycle

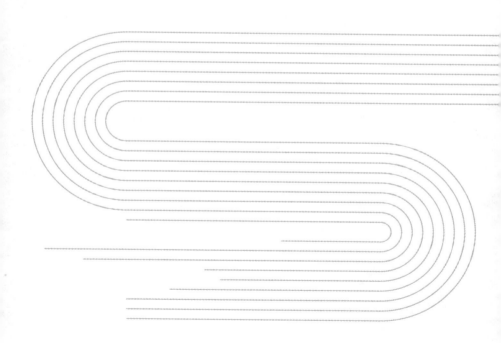

had this picture in my mind of exactly what a professional speaker would look like, how she would carry herself in a room and speak onstage, and it absolutely terrified me. Yet, I felt that professional speaking would be the next natural move in my career, and so I committed to becoming the best speaker I could be in 2020. I chalked the anxiety up to excitement, which I won't discredit, but a big part of it went back to "Can I speak? Will I mess up? Can I show up effortlessly like others do to share my message?"

For months, my thoughts kept me awake at night. I became obsessed with researching how to be the best speaker, how not to forget what I wanted to say, how to nail an interview, and so on. I then went back and forth on whether I should memorize my keynote speech word for word or memorize an outline and hope to fill in the blanks once I got onstage. I spent countless hours swaying back and forth at the kitchen island, rocking my baby to sleep while recording myself reading and eventually reciting my speech. I left zero margin for white space during this time, earbuds cemented to me, replaying my recordings, or mindlessly reciting my speech word for word—no emotion, stoic, and terrified I'd forget a line.

This was not me, the easygoing, off-the-cuff, warm, conversational speaker I usually was, and, ironically, I had spoken numerous times before. But for some reason, with the new-year-new-me mentality that has become so ingrained in many of us, I felt I needed to do better to get bigger opportunities that would skyrocket my career, and I completely discredited the work I had already done. I allowed ambition to lead me to pressure and pressure to worry and worry to perfectionism, which fully engulfed and eventually controlled me. And then, just like that, with what felt like the snap of a finger, our world came to a screeching halt, and all those months of torment and worry were for nothing.

Has something ever consumed you like this? Turned you into a walking ball of nerves searching for anything to bring you peace? You think that talking about the situation might help relieve the anxiety, but nothing you attempt will shake it. You play future scenarios repeatedly in your mind. Each day you add a new scene to the mix until the once minor concern turns into a full-length feature film. The longer you allow the thought to consume you, the more exaggerated you make it out to be, the more fearful you become, and what once was something you could easily hold in the palm of your hand has now turned into a catastrophic event. And when you allow worry into one area of your life, like a weed, it infiltrates, entangles, and chokes all other areas.

Now, what if I told you that most of what you spend your time worrying about will never come to fruition? That season of my life, I wasted months consumed by something that never actually happened. And guess what? I can never get that time back. By giving in to the worry cycle, I quite literally allowed worry and anxiety to consume and steal the life, peace, and abundance God had available for me. Does this sound familiar? Maybe you're in a full-blown anxiety vortex today, allowing the uncertainty of the future to rule over your present day. Imagine the collective of quite possibly days, months, and even years you spend worrying about things that feel significant but essentially aren't. Worry never fixes anything. So you're probably wondering, "If we know how detrimental worry is for our lives, then why do we do it and allow it to steal our peace and joy?"

In this chapter, we will explore the unhealthy love affair we have with worry. We will also explore how to combat the areas of worry in our lives and learn skills that we can use to align ourselves with a life of peace, joy, presence, and abundance.

Why We Do It to Ourselves

So many of us devote our energy and lives to avoiding what potentially could happen in the future. We don't take a trip because we fear our flight could crash. We don't move forward in a new relationship because we are afraid of being hurt again. We pass up career opportunities because we're afraid of not being able to juggle it all. And the list goes on. But what if we jumped out of the driver's seat and learned to surrender our plans and allow God to take the wheel so we can see his beautiful yet sometimes messy plans unfold for us? He never promised life wouldn't be difficult or disappointing, but he did promise that, ultimately, it would all work out according to his plan.

Penn State researchers Lucas LaFreniere and Michelle Newman published a study in 2020 that followed twenty-nine participants with generalized anxiety disorder to see whether their fears materialized over the length of the study.[1]

1. Lucas S. LaFreniere and Michelle G. Newman, "Exposing Worry's Deceit: Percentage of Untrue Worries in Generalized Anxiety Disorder Treatment,"

What they found might surprise you and cement the concept of taking control over your thoughts: Only 8.6 percent of the participants' fears materialized. And not just that, but those whose fears did come true reported that the outcome was not as bad as they had expected. And get this, the most common percentage of fears actually coming true was zero percent. So, ultimately, most of their worries never came to fruition. Can you believe this? We spend our lives worrying about circumstances that most likely never end up happening, keeping ourselves enslaved to fear rather than living God's promise of peace. Living in alignment with God's purpose for your life means taking hold of toxic thought spirals, challenging them, and retraining your mind to replace the lies with God's promises.

Before we get into how to stop the worry cycle, let's chat about why we actually give in to these worrisome thoughts. What it comes down to is control and safety. As humans, we do everything in our power to avoid uncertainty. It pains us not to know what will happen in the next chapter of life, and instead of accepting God's plan, we would rather grasp any little explanation that might be able to forecast what is coming next for us. Now, the narrative we take on is rarely the full and true story. With no way of predicting what God has planned for us, we grab hold of a possible scenario and allow our minds to run with it. By creating this narrative, we are in fact creating safety for ourselves, although a false safety. It feels comforting to envision how the story is going to play out rather than being left in the dark, so we go deeper

Behavior Therapy 51, no. 3 (2020): 413–23, https://doi.org/10.1016/j.beth.2019.07.003.

and deeper into the thought spiral. And before we know it, we find comfort concluding with a false narrative rather than sitting in the midst of uncertainty. But this ends up being a false solution because, as we learned before, over 91 percent of what we worry about will never come true. So as much as we want to obliterate worry, keeping it a part of our lives serves a purpose, keeping us feeling safe and secure. Isn't it mind-blowing how our thought process works? Rather than take a situation day by day and rely on God's truth, we find more comfort picturing a worst-case scenario that provides us with an answer.

This depicts the unhealthy love affair so many of us have with worry. Because painting a mental picture of what could possibly happen provides us with comfort, we continue to walk in worry, as it keeps us secure. It also occupies our minds with something other than uncertainty. Trusting that everything will all work out one way or another leaves too much white space that most of us aren't comfortable with. As a society, we have become so consumed with needing to have each minute of the day filled that peace, space, and open time blocks feel too risky for us. We feel that by manipulating every minute of our thoughts and actions, we are more in control of our lives, which couldn't be further from the truth. There is freedom in allowing life to be spacious and living in the mystery of what God's next steps are for us.

The anxiety I felt that spring was nothing I ever want to walk through again. I look back and see how detrimental it was not only to my own life but also to my kids, my friendships, and my marriage. By being so anxious about 2020 being my career comeback, I was distracted, unintentional in my relationships, short-fused with my kids, annoyed at my husband's every move (poor guy, it's really not the end of the world if he leaves the toilet seat up), and even more frustrated with myself.

So how do we keep ourselves from falling back into the toxic love affair we have with worry? We need to have multiple tactics to choose from.

Consider Professional Help

I want to say up front that if you are struggling with anxiety and haven't had success fighting it on your own, I highly encourage you to talk to a professional. When people ask me when it is the right time to find a therapist, I always respond, "If you've considered it (which you are), find one immediately." Therapy is no longer reserved only for those with clinical disorders; it is beneficial for anyone who is dealing with even low-grade anxiety or depression. Personally, I believe that everyone, big and small, was affected in some way by the year 2020 and that having an unbiased opinion will give you the permission you need to begin healing from it.

God has given clinicians and doctors wisdom in knowing best practices for treating our needs through talk therapy and medication. I do believe that some of us have chemical imbalances and can benefit from medication. I want you to know that taking medication is not irresponsible or Band-Aiding the issue—it is, in many circumstances, necessary for survival. The first time I took an antidepressant, it was as if for the first time in my life my eyes felt fully open. It didn't numb me or instantly remove my problems, but it enabled me to be awake enough to do the work to, first, get myself out of bed and, second, have a clear mind to begin the recovery process by learning effective coping skills. I could finally reason rather than react strictly through emotions. I finally wanted a future and was ready to learn tools to change my behaviors. See the difference? Medication is not a cure-all but a tool to help those who are so deeply in the worry cycle at least stand up so movement can begin. So please use the following tools along with therapy and even medication, if needed.

Examine the Evidence and Rely on God's Word

Overcoming worry begins by examining the evidence around us and challenging our beliefs. In my years of practicing as a psychotherapist, I have found that one of the most effective ways to mitigate the lies we tell ourselves is to replace them with hard evidence. I ask my clients to do this when they express a belief that is most likely being sparked by emotion, uncertainty, and the desire for control. So, for example, someone might say, "I'm afraid to take this next step because I doubt I will be able to keep up. And if I can't keep up, I will fail and end up in a worse circumstance than I am in right now."

So I ask them to go find the evidence that supports this belief. I say something to the extent of "So you are telling me you are rejecting something you so badly want in fear of not being able to handle it once you have it? Can you give me a few examples of times in the past when you were given an opportunity that you really wanted that you weren't able to handle? Or was there a situation in the past that felt impossible to navigate yet you somehow found your way through it?" They typically give me a long list of examples, and then I lovingly reply with, "Hmm, I had a feeling you were going to say that. So how will this situation be any different? This evidence that you've laid out has provided you with facts that you can indeed handle, and even handle with ease, some of the things that had once felt impossible to you. Would you say this sounds true?" I would say that 99 percent of the time, my clients have confirmed that even if a situation didn't work out perfectly, they always found a way to move forward. Often, they just needed someone to reframe the situation for them to understand that even if they were disappointed, they ultimately walked away stronger. Once they can see what I've reflected back, it all clicks, and they can use this exercise each time doubt surfaces.

Christians have even more of an advantage when it comes to searching for the hard facts. Not only can we find personal evidence from our past to back up that we will indeed survive, but we also have the biggest gift available to us at all times for free: God's Word. We can literally flip through Scripture and pick out verse after verse to use to replace the worry and self-doubt. Here's the truth. Exercises like the above can be super useful in challenging our beliefs and worries, but nothing, I say nothing, beats the Word of God. We often forget how powerful his promises are. And rather than getting quiet and sitting in them, we run to everyone and their mother to get advice as short-term fixes for our worry.

So I'm sure you're thinking, "Kate, how did you allow yourself to get so far into the worry cycle that season?" You want to know how? I was doing every exercise I teach in my books and programs. I was processing with all my friends. I hired someone to help me nail my keynote speech. I was consuming books and trainings and anything I could get my hands on to teach me how to rid myself of anxiety while speaking. So why wasn't it working? Well, maybe the better question to ask is, What was I not doing? I had become so consumed with consuming that I neglected prayer, morning devotion time, quiet time, and digging into the Word of God as much as I needed to. I was so obsessed with learning that it clouded my vision of what was right in front of and available to me. I can vaguely remember hearing God say, "Stop leaning in to the teachings of others and lean in to me," but because I had left no margin for life, I quickly ignored him.

Have you ever been in a similar valley? You are consulting everyone but your heavenly Father? You are leaving zero space for margin and the wonder of God? I realized my plan wasn't working, and soon all the world was put on hold with a global pandemic, so none of my worrying about speaking onstage actually even mattered. Talk about a face-palm moment! How hadn't I known better? Well, that's the thing with worry. Most of us do know better, but the Enemy comes to kill, steal, and destroy and knows exactly how to take hold of our minds to distract us and take us as far away from God as possible, convincing us that we have plenty of strength and willpower to do life on our own. So, in order to guard our hearts and minds and protect ourselves from the worry cycle, we must cover ourselves with the armor of God. Ephesians 6:10–18 states,

> Finally, be strong in the Lord and in his mighty power. Put on the full armor of God, so that you can take your stand against the devil's schemes. For our struggle is not against flesh and blood, but against the rulers, against the authorities, against the powers of this dark world and against the

spiritual forces of evil in the heavenly realms. Therefore put on the full armor of God, so that when the day of evil comes, you may be able to stand your ground, and after you have done everything, to stand. Stand firm then, with the belt of truth buckled around your waist, with the breast-plate of righteousness in place, and with your feet fitted with the readiness that comes from the gospel of peace. In addition to all this, take up the shield of faith, with which you can extinguish all the flaming arrows of the evil one. Take the helmet of salvation and the sword of the Spirit, which is the word of God. And pray in the Spirit on all oc-casions with all kinds of prayers and requests. With this in mind, be alert and always keep on praying for all the Lord's people. (NIV)

When worry begins to creep in, we need hard evidence of what God says to replace the lies. Here are a few of my favorite verses to replace worry with truth:

Therefore I tell you, do not be anxious about your life, what you will eat or what you will drink, nor about your body, what you will put on. Is not life more than food, and the body more than clothing? Look at the birds of the air: they neither sow nor reap nor gather into barns, and yet your heavenly Father feeds them. Are you not of more value than they? And which of you by being anxious can add a single hour to his span of life? And why are you anxious about clothing? Consider the lilies of the field, how they grow: they neither toil nor spin, yet I tell you, even Solomon in all his glory was not arrayed like one of these. But if God so clothes the grass of the field, which today is alive and tomorrow is thrown into the oven, will he not much more clothe you,

O you of little faith? Therefore do not be anxious, saying, "What shall we eat?" or "What shall we drink?" or "What shall we wear?" For the Gentiles seek after all these things, and your heavenly Father knows that you need them all. But seek first the kingdom of God and his righteousness, and all these things will be added to you. Therefore do not be anxious about tomorrow, for tomorrow will be anxious for itself. Sufficient for the day is its own trouble. (Matt. 6:25–34)

> Cast your cares on the LORD
> and he will sustain you;
> he will never let
> the righteous be shaken. (Ps. 55:22 NIV)

For God hath not given us the spirit of fear; but of power, and of love, and of a sound mind. (2 Tim. 1:7 KJV)

Assess Vulnerabilities

I know this might sound silly to some, but this next point has played out to be true for thousands of years. The first woman to ever give in to the Enemy's trickery was Eve in the garden after being tempted to eat the beautiful, shiny apple from the tree. We can learn so much from her by pausing and looking at the simplicity of the story. Okay, please don't laugh when I say this, but trust that as a woman, human, and therapist, I have witnessed this at all stages of life, starting straight from the womb—the effect that hunger has on our minds. Have you ever been called hangry? I know my husband gets excited any opportunity he has to pull the hangry card on the three of us girls during a long car ride!

And each time I laugh because I know he's going to say it even before he does.

When people are hungry, their vision becomes clouded and decisions are made from a more emotional state than a logical state. Let me explain. During graduate school, I was trained in Dialectical Behavior Therapy (DBT) and have been practicing it with my clients ever since. One of the big vulnerabilities triggering the use of our emotional mind versus our logical mind is a lack of basic needs. Meaning something like hunger can easily throw us into an irrational thought spiral. And because of this, in DBT, we encourage clients to track their basic needs each day on something called a diary card. This is essentially a weekly chart that captures things such as balanced meals, water intake, sleep, vitamin and medication intake, exercise, prayer/meditation, self-care, physical connection/community, etc. When we lack in any of these areas, we are much more susceptible to be reactive in situations, allowing our emotions to run wild. It can be so easy to forget the importance of fulfilling our basic human needs. Did you know that a lack of food, water, and sleep can even lead to hallucinations? Yep! Basic needs really are that important.

So when we go back to Eve, I get it. Maybe she made a decision out of hunger. Maybe she saw the beautiful, shiny apple, had a craving, was a little more vulnerable because of it, and said yes to sin that would change her life and the trajectory of life forever. So when you find it difficult to reason and the anxiety is beginning to spin out of control, make sure at a minimum you are tending to your basic needs. Personally, consuming over two cups of coffee, which is typically triggered by a lack of sleep, can exacerbate a worry cycle for me. See how important it is that we are aware of how we are treating our bodies? Our bodies and minds are much more intertwined than we think.

Fast for Freedom

Now, for this last point, when I use the term *fast*, I'm not at all speaking about abstaining from food. I know the Bible does talk about using food as a way to fast, but too many women, including myself, have had unhealthy relationships with food over the years, and if you are even slightly near that place today, please don't use food to fast. If food is something you have struggled with, I want you to know that fasting is a heavenly gift that is still available to you. I fast a few times a year, but I have not fasted from food since I was a young adult and not yet aware of my unhealthy obsession with food. Today I acknowledge that using food as my tool to fast would be too risky, so instead I find something else of great value in my life, such as a habit that brings me false comfort. Some of my strongholds past and present are things like consuming too many opinions, social media, overworking in businesses, or time spent in front of a mirror or on a scale. During my recovery breakthrough over a decade ago, I decided that mirrors and scales were not something worth spending hours obsessing over. And during that Lenten season, I gave them up completely. I used a mirror only for essentials like styling my hair or making sure I didn't have a big piece of spinach in my teeth. I stopped spending hours staring at the scale in worry that I might have gained a pound from indulging in the top of a cupcake on my birthday. I also began facing backward on the scale anytime I needed to be weighed by a doctor. To this day, I don't own a scale and love my body more than ever.

I had hated my body as long as I could remember, as far back as four years old, and I had years of my life stolen from me during those first twenty-two years by paralysis, self-loathing, and worrying how people would perceive me. So that Lent I begged and promised God I would do anything for him to take the pain from me. Each time I was tempted to get on a scale or scan my body for every imperfection in the mirror, I cried out for healing and also began thanking him for the future deliverance I knew was on the way.

If worry and obsession are controlling and consuming every minute of your day or even just part of it, please consider giving up something of value for a period of time. I suggest thirty to forty days, as a habit takes a minimum of twenty-eight days to instill. I do somewhere in that range because it's just enough to change my thinking without becoming too reliant on the new habit. So, for instance, after forty days, I didn't go back to the body scanning in the mirror, but I would allow myself to use the mirror here and there with a new healthy outlook.

As you read this, what do you feel God impressing on your heart to give up? Is it a behavior, thought pattern, or relationship that feeds your worry cycle? How would it feel to release this stronghold for a period of time to give you a chance to heal? I pray for you as you enter into your fast that God will reveal a snapshot of the abundance that is available for you. I know for a fact that my healing came through that specific fast, and ever since, other strongholds have been released through fasting.

A Life Free from Worry

I want to leave you with hope and expectancy that God has peace, freedom, and pure joy ahead for you. He never designed us to live shackled to fear and the what-ifs of the future. He came so that we could have peace and a confidence that he is working all things out for us. God has so much for you, sister, and I am begging you today to release your worries. Stop controlling, and stop trying to manipulate what's already been planned. His way is the only way. You just have to trust that peace and abundance are available for you too.

As we close this chapter, I want you to take a few minutes in prayer and meditation and visualize what your life could look like and how you could feel if all your worry and anxiety could be stripped away. Would you be more patient with your kids rather than snapping from the pressure around you? Would you stop dating the wrong guys and believe that God will bring the right one in time? Would you start trusting that God will get you out of your financial mess and give you the energy to find a new job? It is impossible to control or predict the future, but you have full control over how you handle the present. So I invite you to surrender and lay your worries at Jesus's feet today.

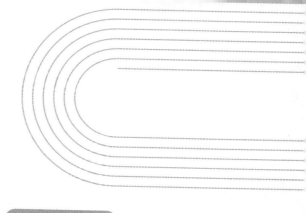

CHAPTER 5

You Don't Need Permission (You're a Grown-Up)

Our first year of marriage I worked the evening shift at our local hospital. The evening shift had its perks, one being a buck fifty more per hour, and the other being not ever needing to request time off for life incidentals such as letting the plumber in or getting to a doctor's appointment. Although being available during daytime hours had its perks, being a newlywed, I preferred not having a schedule opposite that of my husband and friends. Eventually, I found a daytime job, which even gave me weekends off. Score! But I quickly discovered that if I needed to make a doctor's appointment or be home for a repair of the never-ending plumbing issues we had with our 1927 fixer-upper, I needed to learn a new skill called "stating my needs." Going back to the people pleasing chapter, I never wanted to inconvenience anyone at my job. I had experienced firsthand the effects of other clinicians missing work, and it wasn't fun. I began to notice that staff members rarely planned time off but called in the morning saying they couldn't make it to work that day for personal reasons. This left me quite perplexed. Why were this many people constantly missing work without permission? Shouldn't they plan their days off better? I was totally judging, thinking to myself how irresponsible they were being, but little did I know their reasoning and was soon to find out the hard way.

When my husband's sweet grandfather passed away, I needed to take a day off the following week to attend the service. Little naive me knocked on my supervisor's door. "Hey, I need to request Tuesday off for my grandfather's funeral." I should have known better, but this was the moment I learned I would never ask permission again. "But who will cover your groups? You'll need to find coverage. This is a very busy time here, and that will also mean I will need to cover your intake that day. This really isn't a good time. Oh, and sorry about your grandfather." I wasn't going to miss my grandfather's funeral, for goodness' sake, so in this instance, I had no other choice and was forced to do what I had witnessed my coworkers do time and time again. Call the day of the funeral to say I wouldn't be at work.

Looking back, I'm grateful for that unfortunate situation. Knowing what I know now, I certainly would have handled it differently from the start, not asking permission but stating my needs. I am quite confident that if I had exuded confidence in declaring my needs rather than cowering over requesting permission, I would have received a different response. From that day forward, I swore I would do my best to confidently state my needs and no longer allow others to decide for me.

Is this something you struggle with? Maybe . . .

- it's not asking for time off at your job, but maybe you're at the end of your rope caring for the kids all day long and you just need an evening off to lock yourself in the bathroom with a bubble bath, a good book, and a glass of vino.
- you are interested in getting mentored by someone new, which comes with a large price tag, and you feel

like you need the validation of your business friends in order to justify it.

- it's something as subtle as wanting to get a new haircut but not being able to move forward until all your friends approve.

See how subtle yet often permission seeking is capable of being weaved throughout your day?

As we move through this book, I have one very important mindset I need you to grasp. Here it is: You, my friend, are a grown-up, you've earned your badge, and you no longer need permission to pursue the desires of your heart. There is no need to prove yourself or earn permission for what you want in life.

When you go through life asking permission for the little and the big things, you are not really living at all. You are not owning the beauty and the power of personal choice. And I get it. It's so easy to forget that most of the time we actually have a choice and that our choices are not in the hands of others. This mindset is necessary in order to live a life of passion, purpose, and abundance. Alignment doesn't look like doing what you think you should do but rather drawing a line in the sand, claiming your boundaries, preferences, and desires, and then being explicit about where that line falls.

In this chapter, rather than discussing why we ask permission, because I think we can all agree it is rooted in people pleasing—chapter 3 ring a bell?—we are going to tackle the benefits of no longer allowing permission slips to be a part of our lives, how asking for permission actually affects our relationship with ourselves and others, and how we can state and claim confidently what we desire in life.

Tear It Up

How often do you get a permission slip signed? News flash, we aren't in grade school anymore! I can't tell you how many smart and capable women are still asking permission in all aspects of life. Now, I don't think anyone purposefully does this, but it's become a learned behavior from childhood, where choice was maybe not an option for us. But something to keep in mind is just because you weren't and maybe still aren't presented with choices at times, this doesn't mean you don't have choices. You actually get to make a choice in everything you do. You get to choose how you respond to condescending comments from your coworker. You get to choose how you respond to a neighbor who asked you to drive them to the airport for the seventh time this year. You get to choose how you allow your partner to treat you.

You don't need permission to put your foot down. Life can become so much less complicated once we accept "I only need to do what I choose to do." Quite often there is a way around what you think you need permission for. And you, my friend, are smart and capable enough to figure a way around, assert yourself, and state your needs.

Back to the above examples, it's easy to forget that you don't need permission to speak up and call someone out when they are being rude to you. You don't need permission to tell your neighbor that you can't drive them to the airport yet again this year. And you don't need permission from your partner to take some well-deserved time for yourself. Let's get real. Has your husband asked permission to sleep in while you tend to the kids at the crack of dawn on a Saturday? Um, I highly doubt it. He probably just sleeps in and, depending on how you respond, either thanks you after or begs you for forgiveness! So looking at these examples, how often are you asking others for permission that isn't necessary, whether it's asking permission directly from a person or asking others whether they think you have permission to say or do something? You are a grown-up and don't need permission slips. And when you realize that, you will reap certain benefits.

First, eliminating permission slips simplifies life. Period. It eliminates the need for conversations like those mentioned above, the pressure to bargain with yourself, the back-and-forth mental chatter, and the constant doubting whether you made the right decision or if you upset or offended someone. Imagine how easy it would be just to state what you feel is right for you in the moment free from guilt and the pressure of second-guessing yourself? I know firsthand that owning my personal choices without needing permission has made my life 100 percent easier than it was a decade ago.

Second, forgoing permission slips saves you time. How much time have you wasted discussing a potential decision with others when deep down you knew immediately what you wanted and what felt aligned for you? How much time have you wasted going back and forth begging and bargaining with someone to persuade them to grant you permission? And how much time have you wasted in your own mind games second-guessing yourself? When we feel we need permission, we waste a ton of time in paralysis and indecision, always fearful of doing the wrong thing. I recently had to make a hard decision that I knew the other party naturally wouldn't be happy about, and I knew they would try to persuade me otherwise. When entering the conversation, I told myself, "Kate, you already made your decision. Of course they will try to persuade you, but you don't need their permission to walk away. Stick with your no—it will save you time in the end." Former-version Kate would have felt bad and stayed in the partnership rather than realizing she owes no one anything and that if a situation no longer feels in alignment, she has the choice to leave, without permission.

Third, eliminating permission slips instantly elevates your opinion and makes you appear more confident, demanding a higher level of respect. Ever known a wishy-washy person? I am very cautious taking advice from or fully trusting the opinion of someone who doesn't fully believe in themselves. On the flip side, ever come into contact with someone who walks into a room and confidently states what they need? Boldly declaring your needs makes you magnetic. People notice your confidence and want to be around you because you don't need hand-holding. Try it!

Fourth, forgoing permission slips makes you feel like the CEO of your life, your career, your relationships, your business, and your decisions! You feel elevated when you can state what you want without wavering. Have you ever said to someone, "This doesn't work for me," and then walked away beaming with confidence? The truth is that when you state what you want and need out of life, you begin receiving what you want and need out of life. There is a correlation because people begin respecting you and taking you seriously. And guess what? When others begin respecting you and taking you seriously, you begin respecting yourself and taking yourself seriously. See how it's a ripple effect? Each time you are in a place where you need to make a decision, it becomes easier to state your needs because you've experienced positive outcomes in the past. Future decisions are so heavily linked to our past experiences.

Going back to the example of my husband's grandfather passing away, from that day on, I knew I would never ask permission again. I understood that in order to gain someone's respect in the future, I needed to claim it rather than request it. How often do you request respect from others? Does this show up in every area of your life or just in specific areas or with specific people? Have you ever tried claiming it sans permission slip? And if so, how did that go for you?

How Permission Slips Are Affecting You Today

Something I have found fascinating in my coaching career is that many successful entrepreneurs haven't gotten the memo that they don't have to work Monday through Friday 9 a.m. to 5 p.m. This literally boggles my mind! So many have taken on the rules and guidelines that their former bosses placed on them. It always brings me great joy being able to say to them, "Um, you know you no longer have a boss, right? You don't need permission to take a day off. And you also know that you don't have to work 9 a.m. to 5 p.m., right? Not only can you work flex hours and decide what part of the day you want to work, but you can also decide what days and how many hours you'd like to work. News flash, it no longer has to be forty. In fact, if we work together long enough, I'll have you cutting so much of the unnecessary tasks out of your business that you might just cut your hours in half by next year." This conversation is like I've just handed them a limitless credit card and sent them off to Restoration Hardware to furnish their entire home. So many of us are going through the motions believing that we need permission to do virtually anything. Back to that old saying "Don't ask permission, ask for forgiveness." Well, I can't stress the power in this mindset enough! When you begin to realize that you are the CEO of your life and that you get to decide how you want to run the show, life begins to feel a whole lot easier and aligned.

How would you say permission slips are affecting your life today? Are you questioning your decisions? Are you needing external validation to take the next step? Do you feel you really can't move forward until someone else gives you the green light? Living in this mindset keeps you enslaved. When you can't make an executive decision on your own, life feels heavier. You feel reliant on others, and because you need their validation, you also feel compelled to stay on their good side. Remember the people pleasing chapter? When we seek permission, we feel permission is dependent on what we can bring to the other person, which couldn't be further from the truth. And in many ways, this way of thinking can lead to manipulative behavior on our part. Here is how. Going back to my example of requesting time off at work, I used to think that in order to ask my boss for time off, I needed to be on my best behavior and prove I was a serious employee who didn't take advantage of the system. Even though days off came automatically with the job and did not need to be earned, I still felt that in order to use them, I needed to earn them. Can anyone else relate to feeling like you need to prove yourself? Crazy, right? It's not like we are kids checking chores off a chart so we can earn a sleepover with our friends. We've earned the right to make decisions for ourselves, and it is empowering when we decide to accept this truth.

The desire to get permission from others can also backfire and drain them, especially when they are someone who dearly cares for us. Ever have a friend say to you, "Stop asking, of course you can!" or something to that effect? Luckily, if we have good friends in our lives, they will call us out and lovingly challenge us to undo this language. Many years ago, I had a colleague who would come to me looking for permission. It wasn't often, but for some reason, it depleted me mentally when it happened. What pained me the most was knowing how smart and capable she was of finding her own answer just by going inward a bit more, and I so badly wanted her to be able to see this too. This day in particular she came to me to get my opinion on whether she should increase her education. In my opinion, I didn't think she needed to in order to be successful. So I shared this with her, that I believed she already had the skills and just needed to trust herself more rather than invest in something that she felt she needed in order to be successful. I fully believed in her abilities, and this was my honest answer, but it ended up not being the answer she wanted to hear. She felt that I wasn't being supportive of this potential educational advancement and voiced that I hurt her feelings. It was one of those moments when I wanted to say, "If you didn't want my truthful answer, then why did you ask me?" I walked away from the conversation feeling extremely frustrated. From this illustration, can you see how needing permission from others can negatively impact and put a strain on your relationships? Needing permission, especially from those you deeply care about, can be extremely draining for them, putting a heaviness on them, making them feel responsible for your future and your outcomes. I know in that situation I felt a responsibility to share what I felt was true and a pressure that this decision could affect my colleague's life if I didn't speak up. Caring for your own life is hard enough. We need to be mindful not to expect our friends to feel responsible for our destiny along the way as well.

Galatians 1:10 asks, "For am I now seeking the approval of man, or of God? Or am I trying to please man? If I were still trying to please man, I would not be a servant of Christ." God didn't create us to strive for the approval of others. He only asks that we walk according to his will. And this includes respecting ourselves by creating a life that feels free, abundant, and not dependent on others' expectations. Proverbs 19:1 states, "Better is a poor person who walks in his integrity than one who is crooked in speech and is a fool." God wants us to be honest and straightforward in our communication, not manipulative or deceitful. So it goes both ways. It's important that we don't manipulate to get the permission we think we need and that we are open and honest when others ask for ours.

The Big Q

So now that we have the 411 on all things permission seeking, it is time for the big question, my friend. Where do you feel God is calling you? In what area is he asking you to trust yourself more, lean in to this calling, and be obedient with where he is taking you? We started this conversation with all the smaller, less significant things because in order to show up for the divine appointment he has for you, first, you need to be confident in the day-to-day around you. Do you believe that God has a calling for your life that was birthed with you from the beginning of time that you do not need to earn? I sure do. And I believe that God has not given the same gifts to all but has uniquely chosen little old me and little old you to live out a very specific calling. Some of us are called in the workplace to be a light and show his love. Some of us are called to stay home with our kids to do our best to raise strong leaders. Some of us are called to the mission field and the trenches to help those who are suffering. Some of us are called to write from our couches as I am right now. Each of us is uniquely designed to live out a very specific calling, which is shaped by our temperament, personality, upbringing, life experience, and interests.

It brings me so much joy witnessing how very different my kiddos are, even down to the way they developed in my womb, where I could sense their temperaments even before they were born. For instance, my first is strong-willed and pushes the limits. I felt this when she was inside. I said the entire pregnancy she was going to punch her way out early, and so she did, three full weeks early. My second is easygoing, can sit and marvel at books and entertain herself for hours with just a legal pad and a pencil. She was in no rush and hung out almost an entire week beyond her due date. Yep, do the math, pregnant with her almost a full month longer than my first. Ouch. But seriously, how fascinating is this? If this doesn't make it as clear as day, I'm not sure what will. Can't you see how God made you unique even before you entered the world? He had a very special purpose for you from day one that you are prepared for and qualified to live out. You don't need to earn his permission to walk out this calling. He has imparted spiritual gifts from the very beginning, and as Paul tells Timothy in 2 Timothy 1:6–7, he is just waiting for you to fan into flame these gifts and to do so in a spirit of power, love, and self-control. How powerful is that?

Now grab a journal and a pen. I have three questions for you:

1. What do you feel God is whispering to you today? I want you to take a few minutes to dream.
2. What tug have you felt on your heart but have been ignoring?
3. What vision has been imprinted on you since you were a child?

Remember chapter 2, connecting to your heart and intuition? Are you still going back to what you maybe have been ignoring since then? Perhaps you are feeling something right now as you're reading this but are still stuffing your vision down in doubt and uncertainty of jumping too far ahead of this very moment, worrying how all the pieces could even come together. And I get it. Our callings feel risky and scary, and we often feel we need to die a little in order to birth something new. And this is true of anything worth getting in life. So today I want to leave you with a few actions to take.

First, stop waiting for permission from everyone and their mother. Friend, I mean it. God says trust me, not just with some of your heart but with all of it. He reminds us to stop leaning on our own understanding, which causes confusion, and to lean on what he's promised us: "Trust in the LORD with all your heart, and do not lean on your own understanding. In all your ways acknowledge him, and he will make straight your paths" (Prov. 3:5–6).

Second, don't stress about being confident. It might not be there yet, and that's okay! For now, borrow from your heavenly Father. He is our rock, our fortress, and our confidence. We don't need to be any more confident than we are today to take the first step to live out our calling. We need to trust that he will lead the way and pave the path to open doors and opportunity. John 14:26 says, "But the Helper, the Holy Spirit, whom the Father will send in my name, he will teach you all things and bring to your remembrance all that I have said to you."

Third, believe that you will never feel more ready than today. You will also never have more time than today. Waiting has never served anyone. The longer you wait for the perfect timing to arrive, the less ready you will feel. Life gets busier by the hour, and the longer we contemplate our calling, the more time we have to talk ourselves out of it.

And last, as I often say in this book and in real life, give yourself buckets of grace! You will mess up. You will fall back into the trap of seeking permission, but guess what? Each time it happens, you learn. You get right back up and start over. You congratulate yourself for trying when you could have stayed stuck in paralysis. You realize that life is an ongoing lesson and that only practice and time can help you refine what you are trying to accomplish. If you're wondering today if I still ask permission at times, the answer is absolutely! I catch myself from time to time when I'm not walking in alignment but more in the swirl of life. And I immediately course correct. I do what I just instructed you to do. I extend love and grace to myself rather than shame. I get right back up and try again. And each time I fall it gets easier and easier to bounce back. Be gentle with yourself, friend! If no one has told you this recently, you are doing amazing. You really are. And how do I know? Because you are reading this book. You are the 1 percent who are willing to work on themselves. Maybe reluctantly or because someone gave you this book, but you can lead a horse to water, but you can't make him drink. And the same is true for you! No one has forced you to read this book and explore bettering your life. You made that choice and should be so stinking proud of yourself.

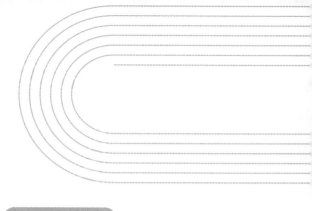

CHAPTER 6

Stop Overcomplicating Your Life—It Doesn't Have to Be Hard

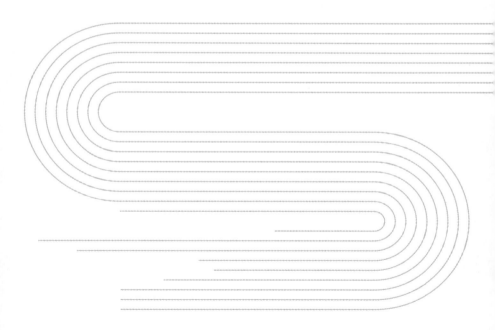

Holidays growing up, I can remember my mother beginning the preparations for family gatherings at least a week in advance. She would start by getting all the dry goods at the grocery store. She not only would set the dining room table with our finest china, crystal goblets, polished silver flatware, cloth napkins, and special decorative napkin rings but also would deck out the table and surrounding room with decorations. Now, this wasn't just Christmas and Thanksgiving. This was New Year's and Valentine's and Easter and any birthdays sandwiched in between throughout the year. The day before the celebration she would slave in the kitchen the entire day making trays of sides that were stored in CorningWare and could easily be warmed up the next day with no trace of food splatters or crumbs throughout the kitchen. She would cook not only a fancy roast, turkey, chicken, or cherry-pineapple spiral ham but also, let me repeat also, a lasagna paired with a gigantic pot of sauce, meatballs, sausage, and shredded beef. My mother picked up this gift of cooking and serving others from her mother. My dad was a pastor, but my parents flipped houses as a side hustle, resulting in us moving quite a bit when we were kids. Luckily, we'd get to live in the new house until they were ready to sell it. So, obviously, each new house would need an extra oven *and* fridge in the laundry room so that all the food could be stored and we would have enough oven space to heat it all up. The day before a holiday all the sides would be ready to go and stored among both fridges. The house would then be scrubbed top to bottom, leaving no trace of evidence that anyone ever cooked in our home. And last, all the pillows would be karate chopped (I know you know what I mean) and all the rugs vacuumed to the point of having those nice vacuum lines throughout the house before we turned out the lights for the evening. I'm pretty sure our current rugs aren't even plush enough to do this in my home. My mom never used an alarm clock, but her internal clock would wake her up at 4 or 5 a.m. to put the meat into the oven and the risen bread dough into the buttered loaf pans. The rest of us would wake around 7 a.m. to the smell of homemade bread cooling, sauce warming on the stovetop, and a roast caramelizing in the oven.

These are great memories that will be forever imprinted on my heart. The amount of love that my mama put into each of these days was enough to fill a lifetime of parties at my house. However, not to sound like an ungrateful human, but it took a lot of therapy for me to undo what was for twenty-plus years ingrained in me as the *right* way to do things. When I moved into my first place and would have friends over for a casual night, I just assumed that all these preparations were what you were supposed to do. Home-making and cooking have never been my love language, although communicating has been, which is a big part of entertaining. In my twenties, I would notice myself coming close to what would look like a panic attack before having others to my home because a picture on the wall was slightly out of place or I didn't have time to bake homemade rolls and had to resort to bakery-bought ones. I would spend hours store-hopping to ensure I had all the *right* things for a proper home gathering. As soon as the guests (I mean my friends) arrived, I would feel so frazzled in the kitchen just like Martha in the Bible when Jesus came for a visit. I would obsess to time everything just perfectly. I mean, come on, I never had my own laundry room, let alone an extra oven and fridge to house food in advance, so I was doing it all pretty much in the moment. The gathering would come and go, and at the end of the evening, I would sit in my kitchen looking at a sink full of dishes, napkins on the counter (paper, of course), un-karate-chopped pillows strewn about, and the beautiful remnants of friends enjoying themselves, yet I would feel empty because I had missed the point of gathering and community. I had completely overcomplicated the entire process because I thought this was how hosting was supposed to look.

What I didn't realize was that for my dear mother, blessing people through food was simply her love language! She preferred to be in the kitchen preparing and found great joy in hearing others compliment the meal and talk about how full their tummies were and having doggy bags of a week's worth of meals (no joke) packed up ready for each guest to grab before they left. I, on the other hand, would sit there and cry because even after following recipe books to a tee, I would still end up drying out, undercooking, burning, or oversalting the food. And like Martha, who completely missed the point during Jesus's visit to her home, I was so caught up in the preparations that I overlooked the big picture—spending quality time with the ones I loved. Unlike Mary, who doted on Jesus and listened to everything he had to say at the house party, I would catch a hello as I collected friends' coats on their way in and a good-bye as I handed them back on their way out. As you can tell, this was completely soul sucking for me, and it took me many years to realize just how detrimental it really was.

The lessons we learn during our developing years are extremely difficult to unlearn, even when we can acknowledge that they are no longer serving us. And many times, rather than assessing whether these mindsets are something we desire to keep alive in our lives, we just go through the motions and continue the thought patterns and behaviors we've learned because we assume they are correct. And when we perpetuate these thought patterns and behaviors because "we've always believed this" or "we've always done things this way," we never quite end up feeling fulfilled, leaving life daunting and burdensome. So many of us are living our lives the way we think we should, need to, or have to rather than how we actually desire to live them. We may also continue these patterns out of guilt. Going back to the family tradition example, for many years, I would tell myself, "My mom worked so hard to pass on these traditions of entertaining, and I must be selfish for not having the desire to keep them going."

Do any of the following examples describe you?

- Growing up, you were taught that success is hard. You watched your parents work multiple jobs just to get by. This left a lasting impression on your small heart. You believe life can't be easy, that you have to strive if you want anything of value.
- You've been following other business owners on social media, and because their branding, photos, website, and videos are so scripted and perfect, you

assume yours must be too or else you aren't doing it right. So you put pressure on yourself to show up with makeup and heels, but everything just feels too hard to keep up with, so you quit.

- All the other moms are allowing their kids to take dance classes four nights a week, and you feel like an uninvolved failure of a mom if you don't do the same. Rather than doing what works for you and your lifestyle, you overcomplicate life because you assume life is supposed to be challenging, and if it's not, you must be slacking or lazy.

Well, I'm here to tell you today that, no, you are not a failure if you are not overcomplicating your life like everyone else in your bubble. You are a grown adult, and you are allowed to have preferences. You are the CEO of your life. You get to write the rules and decide exactly what you want your life to look like. And, yes, if you are overcomplicating it, I promise there is hope for you. It's inevitable that life can be hard, but just because it's hard doesn't mean it can't be ease-filled and enjoyable. In order to live a life that feels life-giving and in alignment with your values, you need to get used to being okay with not overcomplicating things because you think that's how life is just supposed to be.

And in order to live a life of purpose, of abundance, and in line with our desires and callings, we first need to gain insight into how and why we've been overcomplicating things. Then we need to uncover or birth what our version of living in simplicity or, as I like to call it, living a life of ease, looks like to us. Once we can grab hold of that picture, we can begin taking the steps necessary to fully own what it is we truly desire and begin shedding the old beliefs that have kept us overcomplicating things our entire lives.

How and Why We Overcomplicate Things

So if we crave simplicity, why do we constantly overcomplicate things in our lives? I believe a big piece of it stems back to what we heard at a young age. "In order to do well with school, teams, hobbies, and eventually work, you have to work hard. You have to be more dedicated than anyone else. You need to prove yourself to others and stand out." Anyone else hear this? I'm sure you can think back to your childhood, young adult, or early career years and see patterns of unhealthy standards. And as the chapter on people pleasing revealed, we often make things harder for ourselves, knowingly and unknowingly, because we desire to be liked or acknowledged. So why do we overcomplicate patterns and behaviors and how we live our everyday lives? Plain and simple, "Because they said so."

In college, after renting the hit movie *Because I Said So* starring Mandy Moore and Diane Keaton, I began to realize that I had never questioned or examined the why behind much of what I did. I had gone my entire life taking everything that had been taught or told to me at face value. For example, I had even assumed that some of the views shared by Sunday school teachers and Christian school leaders were absolute, such as no sleeveless tops, ear piercings, or PG-13 movies until I officially became a teenager. I trusted that because they were authority figures in my life, if they "said so," it *was* so. And "because they said so," I experienced tremendous guilt when I strayed from what I was told. Now, you may have been fortunate enough to have had an up-bringing where such opinions weren't pushed as hard, and if so, you may not relate as much. But it still is an important reminder for us even as adults to always examine and feel what comes up for us when something is presented to us. And as a reminder, please remember that you have a choice in everything in life.

Take a moment to think back, examine your life, and scan for times when you may have overcomplicated something. Maybe you just did as your boss asked, not thinking there might possibly be an easier way. Or maybe you are living in hustle and bustle because that's just how you think life is supposed to be. Whatever it might be, there are countless examples of how we overcomplicate things.

I was never academically gifted as a kid, so when it came time for internships and first jobs, I held on to some absolutes so dearly because I felt I needed to prove my worth. When I was told to dress professionally, to me that meant being all done up in pantyhose and heels so uncomfortable yet stylish that I'd go home with blisters every night. When I was told to be on time, to me that meant always being the first person to work, even before my boss was there to open the building. I can remember sitting in the parking lot writing to-do lists as I waited for my boss to arrive and unlock the building for me. I kept up a habit pretty much until I left to start my own business of needing to appear busy all the time to show I was a hard worker. So I would take on extra projects, volunteer for things I didn't need to, and have such a full plate that most of the time I needed to work through lunch. I remember for years seeing my coworkers show up on time, take their lunch breaks stress free, be okay with work not being complete yet still leave work on time and so envying their ability not to seem to care. I can remember judging and thinking, "Man, they really don't have a work ethic." Little did I know, they were going about life the right way—not overcomplicating but doing exactly what was asked of them: to work until 5 p.m. I, on the other hand, was making it all so much harder for no reason at all just because I thought that was the way life was supposed to be.

Can you relate at all? Take a few minutes to answer these two questions:

1. How are you making life harder for yourself today?
2. What standards do you feel you need to meet in order to accomplish things the *right* way?

Maybe you have been working so hard to make something happen, pushing a round peg in a square hole and not seeing any results other than frustration, a waste of time, and feelings of defeat, and you are ready for simplicity. Often when we force something, rather than allow a situation to naturally flow, we cause unnecessary harm and damage. Right before having our first baby, my husband and I had a doula come into our home to teach us all the birthing basics to prepare us for what was about to happen. All I can say is thank the Lord we had this woman come. We had no idea what we were in for. The biggest takeaway from that class was that ultimately the baby and mom are safest when no part of the birth process is forced. She pointed out that births that feel traumatic are those in which the process is forced and over-complicated. But when you can prepare yourself to remain calm and breathe through the contractions for as long as you comfortably can in your own home, while keeping yourself hydrated, once you arrive at the hospital, you will pretty much be ready to deliver your baby. Naturally, when those first contractions hit or the water breaks, most women are tempted to rush to the hospital. But if you can sit in the pain, breathe, allow the process to unfold rather than force it, you will have a much more pleasant outcome.

When my water broke with my first child, rather than rushing to the hospital, I had the beach towels ready, ate a nourishing meal of leftover tacos, chips, and salsa, drank a ton of water, finished up my taxes, took a long, hot shower, and then napped for a few hours until the contractions felt unbearable and I was close to delivering. And because we didn't race to the hospital to be forced into all the interventions, we had a much better experience than most people have. Sometimes we just need to slow down, be in the moment, and stop overcomplicating the process. Can you identify times when you were trying to force something rather than finding an easier way?

Design an Ease-Filled Life of Simplicity

So now that we are aware of why we overcomplicate life, it is important that we uncover and identify what exactly we want so that we can begin working toward that lifestyle. Have you ever daydreamed about what your ideal day or life would look like? I'm certain that even those who feel like they're living in simplicity right now could still point out things they'd like to change. When we've been living our lives in the same habits and patterns for years, often it can feel really hard to envision living any differently. I begin with my clients by asking them what they desire less of in their lives. Most can immediately list five to ten commitments, things, and even people they would love to part ways with.

So today I urge you to take some time to complete this next exercise.

1. List five to ten things you are currently doing or that are a part of your life that you want to release.
2. For each one, ask yourself, "Is this something I think I need to do, have to do, should do, or want and desire to do?"
3. Most likely, the answer will be one of the first three statements, and if so, ask yourself why you believe you need to, have to, or should do these things.
4. Where do you feel this pressure coming from? Is it an internal belief deeply rooted from your upbringing, or is it a current external pressure?
5. Ask yourself if it is possible for you to stop doing these things right now. For instance, you can easily and immediately step down from volunteering at the animal shelter four nights a week, but you might have to negotiate with your boss the amount of work you will say yes to moving forward.

Typically, there will be a few things on the list that we have complete power over and can let go of immediately, and then there will be a few things that we will need to work on for some time before we fully release them. Again, some of what you may be letting go of might stem from people pleasing, and you may want to revisit that chapter for some pointers. I also highly suggest looking at commitments on your calendar and tasks on your to-do list each week and then asking yourself, "What are a few things I can cut out immediately that really don't have to be done right away or just aren't serving me anymore?" It's important that we remember something that is available to each of us that we tend to forget, which is choice. We have the ability to choose what to include or not include in our lives. Keep in mind that just because something appears to be a good idea and beneficial to your future doesn't mean it's a good choice for you right now.

So now that you know what you want less of in your life, let's chat more about what an ease-filled life of intentionality would look like for you. When clients sign up to do business coaching with me, they often say they were drawn to my work because my life looks so easy. First, I set them straight and let them know there is a difference between *easy* and *ease-filled*. And then we do the above exercise of removing what no longer serves them so that they can begin building the life they want. I share that the process of creating an intentional, ease-filled life will feel anything but easy. There will be a ton of resistance. The process will feel counterintuitive. All insecurities will most likely rise to the surface. Questioning their worth will also come up, plus so much more. In the next section of this chapter, we will dive into the how of creating an abundant and intentional life, but for now, let's pause to do a little more exploring.

Going back to my clients reporting they want the "easy" life they think I have, I ask them what qualities or aspects they see in my life that they crave more of in their own.

Typically, their answer is this: "The ability to have so much going on, being in the midst of chaos or upheaval, and still not be shaken or fazed." So I ask them to clarify what exactly they mean by this and what exactly they see. They specify that they admire me running my business, producing weekly podcast episodes, writing books, speaking, collaborating, growing other businesses with my husband, spending time with my kids, doing never-ending home renovations and kid-crafting projects, and spending time with extended family. They also report that my life appears simple because I am rarely done up in makeup, am okay showing a messy home on video, and can remain calm when the dog is going berserk over a squirrel outside the window and the kids are quite literally swinging from the chandeliers in the background, often destroying anything I have of value, or hitting each other over the head with Lincoln Logs. So somehow a life of ease to them, in all seriousness, looks like utter chaos to me! However, I get what they are saying because I feel it too. I know that my life is chaotic, I'm ready for the other shoe to drop at any second, but I don't allow any bit of it to shake the deep joy God has placed in my heart. I find little pockets of time to create comfort, peace, and stillness. Even though it's not exactly what society would view as a peaceful life, it is my ease-filled, joyful, abundant, life-giving, intentional life, which is readily available to you too, when you are ready to accept it.

Again, to some, my life may look easy, which is far from the truth—at times it feels really stinkin' hard. I am disappointed a lot. Things never seem to work out as planned. As soon as I feel I can get back on my feet, I'm knocked down again. My kids are all really little, and writing is pretty much the only form of self-care or alone time that I can get in this season. I feel sad that I no longer have spontaneous lunch or coffee dates with friends but rather diaper duty and barf cleanup. I wish that my husband and I could spend more time alone and go out on dates once a week like I see everyone else on Instagram doing. But I have found joy in the midst of it all. A clear depiction of finding joy in the midst of struggles is what Paul wrote while he was in jail: "And I am not saying this because I feel neglected, for I have learned to be satisfied with what I have. I know what it is to be in need and what it is to have more than enough. I have learned this secret, so that anywhere, at any time, I am content, whether I am full or hungry, whether I have too much or too little. I have the strength to face all conditions by the power that Christ gives me" (Phil. 4:11–13 GNT). Although his life felt anything but easy, he still praised God and could find peace in the midst of suffering.

Although my life is not as trying as Paul's, when I endure my own hardships, I am building in a sense of ease through intentionality and choice. Right now in this season, I am choosing all of the above, and along with choosing all of the above, I am also choosing joy, determination, and re-silience when life feels really hard. When making choices, there will always be trade-offs. And by intentionally choos-ing all of the above, the trade-off is not having what I had before kids and a business, which was a whole lot of white space. To experience fulfillment in what I currently have, I consciously decide each day to let down my guard and not comply with perfect while doing the best that I can do with what's available in my hands. Here's the kicker. I can bet you that my life actually is not much different from yours.

Mine in many ways may even be more chaotic than yours. However, the feeling and mindset created around how I am experiencing it are completely different. You might find this shocking, but most likely what you crave more of right now could very well be in your hands already, and by becoming more aware, you will begin to see how much goodness you already have freely available to you.

I purposefully decide each and every day to quit over-complicating life, ditching the belief that it needs to feel easy, and step into finding and choosing joy in the season I am in. See the difference? It's 5:32 a.m. as I am typing this, and I feel so much peace and ease while I sip my coffee and eat my toasted cinnamon bread slathered with butter (fun fact, my family goes through at least two sticks a week) with my cozy slippers and fleece blanket after wrapping up my morning devotional. I am choosing to have a peaceful, uncomplicated morning by engaging in a trade-off: forgoing sleep to wake up at the crack of dawn while the house is still asleep. Intentionality is a choice, and in the search for it, you may have been overcomplicating your process, not realizing that peace and an ease-filled life are available to you if you would just decide to wake up two hours earlier each morning. Two hours earlier could be what's been standing between you, your dreams, and your peace. Can you imagine that? Mindlessly scrolling through social media while bingeing your favorite television show at night rather than reading or journaling or catching up with a friend or getting to bed early so you are rested in the morning is what could be standing between you, your dreams, and intentional living. Yes, I am serious. We tend to blame a lack of fulfillment on our circumstances and how life is failing us. Have a friend who nonstop complains about how hard her life is? You might even be that friend today. When we tell ourselves life is hard, woe is me, and everything is happening to us, life feels really hard, then it becomes hard, and so do our hearts.

Unapologetically Step into Aligned Living

Here's some truth: We often have a lot more freedom and choice than we give ourselves credit for. What if we started viewing life as happening *for us* rather than *to us* and believed that God is always realigning us onto the path he is calling us to? So often things feel hard when we don't have control or don't reap the outcome we desire, but by shifting the paradigm, practicing acceptance, and truly believing that he works all things out for the good of those who love him, we can begin to realize that our lives really aren't so bad after all. Before we go any further into some steps on how to stop overcomplicating life and step into alignment, let me clarify for you the word *acceptance.*

Acceptance is a term that is quite popular in the therapy world, especially in DBT. The belief is that rather than spiraling out of control when life feels out of control, we choose to accept the things that we might not be able to change. Accepting what we can't change does not mean that we are in agreement with it or approve the outcome, but it does mean that we will no longer be held captive by the weight we are carrying by resisting it. Just because I accept that this year was one of the hardest personally for me does not mean that I agree or am happy with the many disappointments I faced, but it does mean that the past is the past, I'm moving on, and I'm working on what I can control in my life. With that being said, the first step of living an aligned, full, and abundant life is practicing acceptance when things suck and feel really hard.

Second, to quit overcomplicating things and begin making things feel easier and more aligned, we need to ditch perfectionism. There is no way to live an ease-filled life when we are focused on things being perfect. Perfectionism robs us of what's available for us. Perfectionism makes what we have never enough. Perfectionism leaves us feeling empty. And perfectionism keeps us paralyzed. When we set our standards so high, they feel nearly impossible to attain and maintain. So what happens? We freeze. We stop. We quit what we set out to do because it will never measure up anyway. When we make things hard, we set ourselves up for failure. This is why patience with ourselves and a good pace in the process are so important. When we make things hard, we fall off the wagon and don't follow through on our commitments to ourselves and others. Here's an example. When you haven't been to the gym in months and then commit to going seven days per week, you are only setting yourself up to fail. This is why it's critical you release perfection and embrace the right pace by asking yourself, "What can I realistically commit to? One or two days per week to start?" See the difference? By setting realistic expectations and knowing your limits, you will follow through on what works for you rather than what you think you're supposed to do.

This is the essence of ease that my clients report wanting to take from me and bottle up—the simplicity of only giving what we have and doing what we can with what's available to us at the moment. If I waited for perfect to show up in my business, with hair and makeup done, a styled outfit, no kids running amok in the background, I would be waiting forever. Luckily, I cracked the code a while back and have committed to showing up with whatever my circumstances are. No one will care about the mess in the background when they desperately need your message. It's about surrendering ego and selfish expectations to be fully available for whatever you are trying to be present for, whether it's your boyfriend, your girlfriends, or the small group you lead. Your boyfriend doesn't care that you wore the same outfit yesterday. Your girlfriends don't care that you haven't had your eyebrows groomed in ten months (true story). And your small group isn't going to judge you for running through the McDonald's drive-through for your kids' dinner tonight. Why are you overcomplicating things? No one actually cares. By living in perfectionism, you are only robbing yourself of the abundance God is holding out, begging you to receive.

Third and last, to create an ease-filled, aligned life free from the expectations of self and others, you need to take ownership. You need to become unapologetic in stepping into the CEO role of your life, family, career, business, friendships, and opportunities. You need to remember that you write the rules. You get to create a life as over- or as undercomplicated as you want. Going back to our opening example, as the CEO of your life, you get to decide if you want to stress out over cooking the perfect meal when friends come over or if you want to make it easy by asking them what their favorite take-out meal is and ordering it when they arrive. Yep, I just said that. Since having kids, we made the conscious decision that if our home hosting standards were too high, we would never see our friends. So 85 percent of the time when we invite friends over, it's on a whim and it's to get their favorite take-out meal. Do you think they care that we are eating with wooden chopsticks instead of with hand-polished sterling silver flatware? I doubt it. What they care about is being able to keep life simple and be in community barrier free, even when life feels chaotic. What decisions or areas of your life can you begin to take ownership of today to create simplicity, intentionality, and more purposeful connections?

So what's possible when we can release our unrealistic expectations of ourselves, surrender, and step into ease? Going back to the "force-versus-flow" concept, a while back I worked with a client who was experiencing resistance in her intimate relationship. She and her boyfriend were trying everything to make the relationship work, but there was constant friction. She was mentally exhausted and was no longer living in alignment with what she had envisioned for her life. And to cope, she began to throw herself into her work. She knew things had to change. She had created her business for freedom and ease, and now she was using it to distract herself from the chaos. Over time, we discussed how this was affecting her, and she boldly decided to end things with him. She knew she was ready for a relationship that didn't feel hard. And so I suggested that she write down an unfiltered list of everything she wanted in a partner. I know you single ladies may be rolling your eyes at this exercise, but don't knock it 'til you try it, and never lower your standards, girls! Less than one month later, an incredible man entered her life who embodied almost everything she recorded on her list. This relationship didn't feel hard. Life began feeling whole and abundant again. Over the next few months, she reported just how ease-filled life felt and how she was no longer pushing against resistance. She loved her life so much that she no longer felt the need to throw herself into her work. Her focus became *living*, and her business purely became an extension of that (as it's supposed to!). She shed blinders as she looked back at how she had overcomplicated things as a way of trying to control life. She then acknowledged she had had a choice all along. Yes, suffering and setbacks are bound to be a chapter or two, but today she can choose to live and run her business from a place of ease. She realized she could take ownership, step into the CEO role of her life, and intentionally choose her next steps.

Are you ready for this today? Are you done making life so hard for yourself? Are you ready to begin accepting what life throws at you, resisting perfectionism, embracing the right pace, taking ownership, and stepping into the CEO role of your life? Stop overcomplicating what God has given you, accept what is available, and embrace the ease he is holding out for you to grab hold of today.

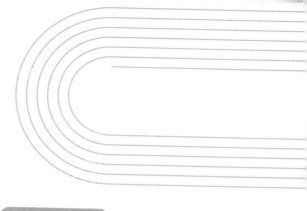

CHAPTER 7

Bet on Yourself

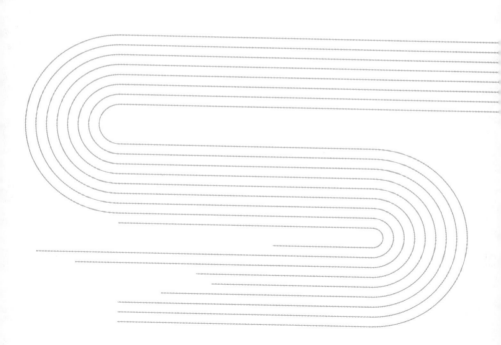

Our 2018 Martha's Vineyard annual family beach vacation was filled with massive joy, yet excruciating angst. Day one was a picture-perfect beach day—just enough warmth from the June sun to make you sweat yet a refreshing breeze that could cool you right off. If you've been to the Cape in June, you know exactly what I mean! Annabelle was just a year old, and I was somewhere around four months pregnant with Charlie. The rest of the family was already en route to enjoy a morning at the beach, while the hubs and I had stayed back to discuss a writing schedule during our time there so I could work on refining my book proposal. Just weeks before, I had signed with my literary agent (lifelong dream!), and because I was eager to secure a book deal before having my second child, I felt an immense internal pressure to have it done yesterday. This opportunity felt like a ticking time bomb, and I so desperately was trying to protect myself from what had gone haywire during my first maternity. Let's just say I had a very hard time adapting to what felt like the loss of my business. If you're interested in reading about that season of my life that I spent on the hot-mess express train, go ahead and pick up my first book, *Thinking Like a Boss*, and turn to chapter 7. I promise you'll feel better about yourself after reading about me!

Well, this conversation with my darling hubs didn't go as planned, and a good two hours that I could have spent on the beach adding some sun to my pasty legs or refining my book proposal were spent arguing about how I wasn't feeling as supported in this process as I had hoped. Let's just say some not nice words were spoken (mostly by me). Pregnancy hormones are no joke, and besides that, I can get, well, um, quite passionate when I believe in something and will go to all measures to accomplish what I've set out to do. Maybe it's the Italian in me, or some say I'm an Enneagram 3. Who knows! But I got so passionate in pursuing this goal that I may or may not have threatened to exclude my husband from the acknowledgments section of the book once it was published. Okay, I confess. True story. I know I'm not alone! You have probably 100 percent felt an immense passion about something before. You've experienced an adrenaline-filled conversation or have written your feelings down on paper and maybe crumpled it up after feeling embarrassment or shame over some of what you wrote. It can be difficult when it's you against the world, often trying to prove something that no one else will understand the way you do but, ladies, embrace it. Also, sidenote: If you are in a relationship and begin to resent your partner or feel communication isn't working, couples therapy works wonders! This was certainly a painful point for us, but we can now look back and laugh at the things "Kate has regretted saying while pregnant."

And so I want to talk to you today about the power of letting it all go (cue song as the kids are watching *Frozen* in the background), surrendering, leaning on God like it's your job, and accepting that no one but your heavenly Father can fathom that dream that's on your heart. And when you can stand firmly planted with an unshakable confidence, you won't need anyone but yourself to bet on you. When you know without a shadow of a doubt that your dream was implanted in your heart because it was for you, walking in alignment looks like bulldozing ahead despite a lack of support or understanding from those who love you.

As you may have learned by now, a majority of the pressure we feel is mostly placed on us by us. Ironic, right? Writing my first book was a huge risk. I would ruminate more often than I'm proud of and wonder, "What if all this work leads to nothing and I someday regret the time I spent chasing this dream?" That week on vacation I so badly wanted to dive into my work (guilt free) to prepare for pitching to publishers, but instead I felt excruciating guilt and resistance—believing I was disappointing my husband and family by needing to sneak away to write. I would ask myself constantly, "What if all this is for nothing? What if the last ten months of pursuing this book idea were a complete waste of time because no one will actually want to buy my book and I will have wasted time that could have been spent mothering my newborn or having quality time with my husband?" All those insecurities surfaced, and my own pressure grew by the minute. At the moment, no one else could see the big picture like I did. Even though friends and family loved me and cared about my future success, there was no way for them to feel the sense of urgency I felt. However, in this urgency, I had a sense of peace and confidence that although my dream felt out of reach, and although I feared I was disappointing everyone, I knew deep down my plan would work. Although I was confident in my plan, I still felt a sense of loneliness that tugged at my heart. Was I the only one who believed in this dream yet again? Several years prior, I had been in a similar place while launching my first two businesses, feeling as though I was the only one who truly believed in the vision. And maybe I was. But guess what? I quickly learned that I would be okay.

Today you may not be threatening to exclude your husband from the acknowledgments section of a book, but you may be fighting your own fight.

- You've decided to pursue your music career in addition to your corporate job, and no one seems to understand why you need to dedicate every Saturday to practicing.
- You've decided to start a nonprofit, and it feels like an uphill battle trying to recruit volunteers and get your friends to understand your time away.
- You've decided that in addition to homeschooling your young kiddos you would like to start your own wellness business via a direct sales company.

Each of these examples is quite different yet yields one common denominator: betting on yourself. You know you could live a very simple life doing what you've already been doing, but you feel that tug on your heart that God is calling you to do more. You may not see the full picture today, but you can see a light right in front of you to help you take the next right step. Living a life of alignment is about taking bold action to bet on yourself and your dreams as you step into the God-appointed calling that is waiting for you.

What exactly do you need to do to bet on yourself? First, you need to make what you want a priority. So often we say we want something badly, yet our actions don't quite match up. We say we want to leave our job to start a nonprofit, but after work we go home and binge television rather than do the research to get it going, making our actions incongruent with our words. Second, you need to take bold, calculated risks, the kind that only you will understand and others will question. Years ago, I heard someone say, "Your dreams are too small if no one is laughing at them." I realized in that moment that I had been playing it safe in fear of receiving disapproval from others. It was like a light switch flipped. Immediately, a boldness was turned on, and from that day forward, I've sworn to live by it. Third, you need to have faith as you navigate the messy middle, as I like to call it, that place right between what we hope for and what we now see, and the desert seasons.

Set Your Priorities

I can't tell you how often I have this conversation with women. "But, Kate, I just don't have the time to pursue my dream. I'm just too tired and don't have the brain space to add one more thing, even though I'm miserable and can't stop complaining and annoying everyone around me because I've been all talk for years with starting this venture." Ouch. Yeah, this might be you. And you might be sitting there wanting to slam this book closed, chuck it across the room, and never hear my name again. I get it. The truth hurts! But I'm here to lovingly hold up a mirror and show you how you've been massively getting in your own way and saying that this dream that would finally bring peace, abundance, and fulfillment to your life is just not a priority today. And this doesn't quite add up. Friend, if you want something bad enough, you'll find the inner gumption to do what maybe doesn't feel like comfort but will get you steps closer to finally betting on yourself. Again, we can talk about our goals with our therapist, friends, coworkers, family, coach, and pastor until we are blue in the face, but if we don't actually make those goals a priority, we are wasting time and breath.

Over the years, I've developed a personal boundary. If I care about someone and catch them talking about a goal but they are clearly allowing excuses to take the wheel and they sound miserable, I will flat out tell them, "If this really means that much to you, you will do something about it right now. I love you and I refuse to have this conversation with you this time (again) next week, month, or year. End of story." Many years ago, two other boss mom besties and I rented a house in Colorado to retreat and spend time brainstorming for one another's businesses. One of the mamas shared about something that had been getting in the way of her potentially doubling her business income, and I gently said to her, "I love you. I have heard you talk about this for a while now, and it's clearly not serving you. I can tell you want to move forward. You see the benefits beyond the fear. Imagine how good it would feel to run through the fear, prioritize that goal, and make it happen. Please, no more talking about it. I want to see you begin taking action. Okay?" I'm sure my words stung a bit. But, guys, guess what? She decided to stop playing it safe and take scary action to bet on herself and do the work, and she has since tripled, I think even quadrupled, her program enrollment! We always come back to that pivotal conversation to celebrate each time she relaunches and her business grows. Often it feels lonely when we are betting on ourselves, but what if our friends and family are just tired of hearing us talk? So the first step to betting on yourself is making your God-given dream a priority.

Now, I'm sure you are wondering, "But how? I've tried so many times, and I just can't get it together." Well, my first two books go deep into different ways of "getting it together," but for the sake of not wanting to repeat myself, I am going to leave the in-depth explanation to the other books and share only what I want you to immediately begin doing: waking up early. "Oh, come on, Kate. That must be easy for you." I know this might push a button for you, but again, I am not here to be liked or to gain your approval. I am here to challenge you to ignite change in your life, friend! So let's chat about how we can shift our behavior and begin putting action behind our dreams so they actually come to fruition.

I had a realization several years back while admiring friends who were consistent with either carving out quiet time in the Word or getting a workout in. I swear they were onto something! And so I began to notice one thing these friends had in common: completing these activities before their workday started. By making something a priority first thing in their day, they were more apt to keep the habit alive and there was less of a chance something would interrupt their plan. So the lesson here is if you want to make something happen, do it *first*. Things like our jobs, cooking dinner, taking the dog for a walk, and showering are things we have been trained to do on autopilot. I don't think any of you would just snooze your alarm seven times and not show up for your job, right? You've been trained to get yourself ready (sometimes reluctantly) and just go. And so for goals and desires that are a little more difficult to instill, I suggest doing them first thing, and here is why.

With our words and actions, we are claiming that this task is the most important thing at this moment, so we will give it our best. If you are a morning devotional kind of gal, I would continue doing devotions when you wake up, as you are declaring that God is your number one priority and that all other goals come next. Then, before the news, the emails, or the checking of social media, do what is next in priority for you. By putting action to your words and making something a priority instead of just saying it's a priority, you are showing a commitment to God and yourself that you are all in.

I understand how hard it can be when the bed is warm and the air is cold and you're overtired and overworked, have toddlers or teenagers, or are living through loss. I get it. It's *hard*. And I do warn you that waking up early never gets easier—it feels just as daunting morning after morning. But what I find helps the most is having something small to look forward to, something that brings me joy that's ready for me immediately when I wake up. Then, when that alarm begins obnoxiously beeping in my ear, I have the motivation to jump up and get started. For some, this reward might be a hot shower with your favorite soap or a bowl of your favorite breakfast cereal. I prep the coffee the night before so that as soon as my feet hit the ground, I can push that little button and in under three minutes I have a cup of hot, delicious coffee in my hands. I can't stress the importance of finding that small thing that sparks joy and having it ready for yourself immediately. This will make all the difference. And who cares if you need a special incentive to accomplish your goal? Do what you can to make it work!

And if you need more incentive, visualize the positive and the negative. Keep in mind you may need to do this every day for years before something begins to feel more like a natural habit. Think about how you feel when you snooze your alarm seven times and don't have enough time for what you desire to be a priority for you. It feels awful! Okay, now hold on to that feeling of disappointment in yourself. Next, visualize how amazing it feels to jump up at the sound of your alarm, declaring your goal a priority, achieving what you set out to do all before actually starting your day. Oh, it feels divine! Well, my friend, that's what living in alignment feels like. You have a sense of pride because you have done something hard that most others don't want to do. You know you are taking baby steps toward something really important to you. And you know that in time you will be further along than you were yesterday. This is what living a life of alignment is all about.

Keep in mind that prioritizing so that you can begin feeling more aligned in your actions should happen not only with professional or personal goals but also with relationship goals. When I had my first baby, I was finding it really hard to keep up with one of my besties. By the time she would get home from work at night, I would be passed out in the nursing chair. So what did we do? We switched our phone dates to 6 a.m., before she went to work and before the baby was up. Prioritizing our time together felt so special and brought us closer.

So the next time you have a goal that is important to you, prioritize and make sure you give it your all first thing and not the leftovers from your day, okay? You know exactly how you feel after a long day at the office. You know how little energy you have after chasing toddlers around the yard and peeling them off the neighbors' fence to get them to take a bath before dinner because they may or may not have rolled around in something that wasn't a pile of dirt in your yard. Yeah, envision that. The mindset and level of patience you have at the end of that whole debacle are not going to be the same peaceful mindset and level of patience you would have shown up with before the day even started. Make sense? I don't know about you, but I'm typically at the end of my rope by 4 p.m.!

Take Bold, Calculated Risks

In my early twenties, before getting married and having kids, I lived quite a "cushy" life, or what I thought a cushy life entailed. I'd wake up, dress up with heels and makeup, grab coffee at my favorite Upper West Side coffee cart on the way to work, settle into work, on a good day break with my co-workers for lunch, and then wrap up around 5 p.m. Gym bag in hand, I would hop on a subway and travel several stops past my apartment to my favorite gym. There I would do a light workout, but really I would just go for the spa-like experience with eucalyptus towels provided post-workout and showers and dressing rooms fully stocked with the most luxurious bath and body products. Then I'd hop back on the subway and either grab takeout or whip something together from the frozen food aisle at my favorite local market. It would then be around 8 p.m., and I'd have the rest of the night to relax, read, watch my favorite shows, and so on! On weekends, my now husband would visit, and we would leisurely walk the streets of New York City looking for fun places to eat, grab groceries at the local farmers' market, meet up with friends for a drink, meet up with some more friends for another drink, and meander back home when-ever we felt like it without a care in the world. Back then my mom would tell me, "Just enjoy life. Travel. Take your time. And really, kids are not for everyone. Think hard before you commit to kids. There is so much out there." Now, I love my mom dearly, and she completely meant this from a place of "Your life is simple, and kids are messy and can hurt your heart at times." It was from a place of wanting to protect me from pain. But keeping life "simple" or not risking pain simply equates to playing it safe.

I had a great life back then. Granted, I lived paycheck to paycheck, had zero savings, and wasn't afraid to purchase nice things that I liked, even if I had to put them on a credit card. Looking back, despite the appearance of a simple, cushy life, my life was actually quite risky. I was dependent on someone else for a job. I was just making my bills each month. I had zero retirement or savings and was drowning in student loan debt. Thank you, Columbia University. I had a landlord who could decide to jack the rent up at any time he wished. Yet, to me, it appeared I was playing it safe. I can't tell you how often I hear the following from women: "I could never leave my job to start a business, because what if I failed?" "I could never purchase real estate for fear of the market crashing." "I could never be a mother because I'd risk losing my career, my dreams of traveling, my flourishing social life, and even my identity."

What if I told you that betting on yourself and stepping into full alignment means taking bold, calculated risks? Calculated risks, you ask? Yes, those audacious risks that, although there's a chance of the situation going completely sideways or dying, if it did work out even just a little bit, would be fully worth taking. And when I talk about taking a risk, it's not just about throwing spaghetti on a wall and praying it will stick. It's about calculating all angles, the pros and cons of winning and the pros and cons of losing. Yes, every little scenario must be carefully thought through. I'm not going to bore you here with a discussion on decision-making. I could write an entire chapter about it, which I've actually done in my first two books. But for the sake of time, we will dive specifically into how we can bet on ourselves.

Maybe you're thinking, "I can't take a risk now. I've lived my entire life comfortably." And maybe you have, but I bet underneath what feels and looks like comfort there is evidence of you betting on yourself! What we want to do today is find little bread crumbs of evidence to show you that you in fact have already taken bold, calculated risks and you are capable of taking even bigger ones in the future in hopes of stepping into a more full, robust, and abundant life of alignment.

One of my favorite books on risk-taking is *In a Pit with a Lion on a Snowy Day* by Mark Batterson. The entire book centers on one small verse in the Bible, a story that has been easily overlooked yet packs a huge lesson for us about taking bold, calculated risks. Second Samuel 23:20 tells the story: "Benaiah son of Jehoiada, a valiant fighter from Kabzeel, performed great exploits. He struck down Moab's two mightiest warriors. He also went down into a pit on a snowy day and killed a lion" (NIV). Wow. I am afraid to walk my dog for fear of slipping on some black ice on our perfectly flat driveway on a snowy day here in New York. Can you imagine choosing to climb down into an icy pit, sans protective gear and modern-day weapons, just your bare hands, maybe a rock or a spear, and risking your life to kill a lion? No way. But to Benaiah it was worth it. This man trusted God and bet on himself.

I think of Noah working on the ark for almost eight decades, being mocked, called "off his rocker," and dismissed as the kooky uncle Noah who believed in conspiracy theories. Man, it must have been brutal for poor Noah. We can learn a lot from the unshakable faith Noah had as he endured years of ridicule yet followed through on the mission God placed on his heart. This man trusted God and bet on himself.

And then there's Esther, one of the boldest women in the Bible, who was willing to risk her life to save her people. She couldn't even ask her husband, the king, a question without his permission. Years leading up to this moment, God had been preparing her. He gave her favor, placing her in the palace for this very mission. Esther knew God had a call on her life and a very important mission for her to accomplish. Despite the uncertainty, she was willing to bet on herself, and because of this, God blessed her obedience and spared her people from being executed. She could have lived the cushy, protected life of a queen, but she knew that risking it all would be worth it.

Talk about courage. I can barely risk signing up for a spin class at the gym for fear of being too out of breath and potentially needing to leave the class early. Can you even imagine chasing down a lion in an icy pit, pouring seventy-five years into building an ark without a drop of rain, and risking quite literally life as a queen to bet on something you believe in and see possible for the future? Friends, there are many other Bible stories about others who listened and answered the call, were obedient, and saw great abundance by not allowing fear to hold them back from God's plan. These people were not fearless. They struggled. They went back and forth with their emotions. I'm sure they doubted and wanted to quit, but they knew their actions would be worth the risk and did them anyway. They knew that a life of safety was anything but safe. And although you may not feel it today, I can guarantee you have been in their shoes in smaller ways your entire life leading up to this very moment. You are probably thinking right now, "Kate, there is no way I've ever taken risks like these characters. I can barely find the courage to make an appointment with my boss to talk about getting promoted in the future." But here's the truth. Just like Esther, you have been preparing your entire life for this very moment without even knowing it. I am going to take you through a rather quick exercise to lay out the evidence and prove to you that you are prepared and ready to bet on yourself so you can take some bold, courageous steps toward what you really desire in life. So here we go!

Here are a few scenarios to get your mind going.

- First think back to childhood, where I'm sure you had some fears around trying out for a sports team or humiliating yourself onstage in a hot-pink tutu. And I bet you still tried anyway, right?
- Now think back to middle school. Maybe it felt risky to go away to summer camp or to ask the new girl if she wanted to sit with you at lunch. But I bet you still did it anyway.
- Now high school. This was at the peak of risking humiliation. Maybe you really liked that tenth-grade boy, and so did all the other girls. But you decided

when he asked you out to say yes, even though saying yes meant opening yourself up to judgment and jealousy. But something told you it might just be worth the risk.

- Now think about visiting colleges and choosing a place you would be shipped to with a bunch of people and even a roommate you'd never met before. But you decided your career destiny and chose the path you would take by claiming a major.

I know your story may have looked a bit different, but I'm sure you encountered scary decisions, and I have a feeling you made them anyway, correct? I could keep going, but I'd like to give you the opportunity to search for the evidence yourself. Often we need to hear someone else's memories to get ourselves back to ours. So now that you've heard some examples, take about ten minutes, beginning in your childhood and arriving at where you are today, and list all the ways you have in fact taken bold, calculated risks. It could be quite easy to gloss over this exercise, but I'm begging you to do it. This is what will set you up to see just how capable you are at taking more bold steps to help you grasp what you truly desire in life.

Have Faith as You Navigate the Messy Middle and the Desert Seasons

Betting on yourself requires you to have faith in the messy middle: the place right between what we hope for and what we now see (Heb. 11:1). The messy middle can be extremely painful as you witness what you've hoped and prayed for slip out of your hands, often with zero warning or context. In the messy middle, life becomes one long, never-ending swirl of a day in which you convince yourself that pausing is not an option or you will risk losing steam, momentum, and what you have worked so hard for. This is the place many of us grow frustrated with God and begin to doubt. But God is using this messy middle to prepare you for your assignment. Clarity, breakthrough, and vision can only surface once everything has settled. You can only reason once you are out of the so-called swirl of life, and then you will see how each season has been preparation for the next. I can't tell you how many messy middles I've been in, but after the abundance I have seen afterward, I would never take any of them away. Have you been in the messy middle recently? Or can you relate to this season today?

Now, I hate to break it to you, but what arrives after the messy middle in many ways is the most torturous season of all. It's the place we feel we're floundering and searching for anything we can find to grab hold of, yet we see absolutely nothing. I think of Noah. I bet at first he felt the urgency to get started on the ark. And then it probably felt like hit after hit when people taunted him, called him crazy, questioned his judgment. And then year after year and decade after decade passed with a literal drought, no flood, and no sign of God working. Despite everything, he kept going in anticipation of God coming through. The messy middle is a place we can typically power through, keeping our focus on hope and an end in sight, but in the desert places, like the one Noah faced for decades, things can feel quite defeating and even unbearable. Although the chaos of the messy middle is not ideal, it is more comfortable than the desert because there is still movement—maybe messy movement, but movement. I don't know about you, but I'm quite a pro at running on skimped sleep, caffeine, adrenaline, with a long to-do list, but what I'm awful at is sitting, waiting, and being patient for what I hope will arrive. I would take all the chaos and running any day over sitting around twiddling my thumbs waiting for the okay from God to move forward.

During the waiting, you may feel like you have failed. Like Noah, you are in a season of drought in the desert. You did the work, you took all the consistent action, and yet still nothing is happening. And then you wonder if it was all worth it. You find yourself questioning . . .

- Maybe my family was right and it was a dumb idea to start a business.
- Maybe I'm really not cut out for this career and there is no hope of moving up in the company.
- Maybe my writing really does suck and I wasted all that time away from my kiddos that could have been spent making memories. Now the only memory they'll ever have is of Mom trying and failing.

Friend, I've been there. Trust me. Desert seasons are the hardest of them all. Somehow, as humans, we have learned how to survive and make it to the next day in the messy middle, even when life is unraveling, but in seasons of stagnation and waiting, we absolutely crumble. But what if God was bringing you through the desert season to grow and develop your patience and character? Or what if God is allowing you to *rest* so that when *his* plan unfolds, you will be ready to act in obedience and *run*? What if I told you that desert seasons are just as necessary as seasons of running? Our bodies need rest. We weren't made to work and serve around the clock. Even God rested on the seventh day. What I want you to learn in this chapter is that quiet and stillness do not equal failure. We can't rush our success. Learning to wait our turn is a skill necessary for survival. In order to bet on yourself, you need to find a confidence in Jesus that is so pure you won't doubt one bit that what you're doing is correct. You can feel it deep in your bones and, like Noah, are willing to sit and wait decades if that means winning your bet.

Recently, I did a unit with the kids on bears. Boy, did I learn a lot teaching a two- and three-year-old about hibernation. I felt God gently nudge me that maybe this lesson was more for me than for them. What I heard was that we need to clothe ourselves with the confidence of bears. A bear doesn't question his season of hibernation. He doesn't ask, "Will I miss out all those months on some good food or opportunities to hunt?" No, the bear trusts and instinctively knows that in order to survive the coming seasons, he must pause to rest. And if the bear lost trust in himself and decided to wake, wander, and search for food during hibernation, he would be putting himself at risk from the elements and possibly starvation by expending too much energy. Bears require this season of rest to conserve energy for the destiny ahead of them.

Can you just picture having the mindset of a bear? Being so trusting in yourself and God's plan for your life that nothing could shake that feeling? Imagine being at peace with seasons of not getting one bite on that dating app or one call back on your résumé. Imagine having so much confidence in yourself and God's plan for your life that bringing zero income into your business as you pursued a separate calling felt so right. Betting on yourself is learning to embrace the hurry up and wait of life. I get all kinds of feels when I hear this term. I can still remember the first time I ever spoke to a professional about what a writing career entailed. She warned me, "Kate, I know you and your eagerness to make things happen yesterday. I am going to tell you that this industry from start to finish will be the biggest hurry up and wait you'll ever experience." I thought for sure she was joking until I began to pursue the process, and, boy, was she right—as soon as you feel you've rushed and scrambled to arrive to the next place, it's time to wait again. But here's what else I realized through this experience. Isn't everything worth betting on a hurry up and wait? I can't think of anything that felt worth it to me that did not feel like an excruciating wait.

So how do you navigate the messy middle and the desert seasons?

First, practice acceptance. Accept that life might not feel ideal today but that every moment is leading you to your ultimate destiny. Accept that God has designed each of the seasons so intricately to serve the next and that they are necessary for you to gain the strength for what's to come. Without the energy drain of the messy middle, we would completely lose our minds in the times of waiting and feeling as though nothing is happening. But what God is doing in this season is recharging us, allowing us to rest up and get ready to run our race, which will appear when his time is right. And by accepting rather than fighting this season, we can learn to just lean back and rest in his love.

Second, embrace the desert, get quiet, lean in, listen for what the Lord is trying to reveal, observe deeper, and most of all *rest*, because the floodgates are about to open. This desert season is what is molding you into who you need to be for the run. The year of the global pandemic I knew that life would eventually go on, childcare would reopen, and I would have an opportunity to dive back into my career. When it felt excruciating to sit in limbo, I reminded myself of those bears in hibernation and how God was giving me an opportunity to rest in his arms, still be taken care of, and conserve energy for the run ahead.

Third, release the outcome. Often when we bet on ourselves and take bold, calculated risks, we fall absolutely flat on our faces. What you need to remember in those instances is that God has brought you through to show you something better. His ways are always better than ours, and he brings us through lost opportunities to show us what is really available for us. I'm sure that Esther, Benaiah, and Noah all realized that betting on themselves and taking bold action could result in mockery or even death, yet they released the outcome and allowed God to do his thing.

And last, embrace the duality of life each step of the way. I know it's not always easy to see, but what look like seasons of stagnation are also seasons of growth. What look like seasons of heartache are also seasons of redirection. What look like seasons of pain are also God stripping away pride from your life. And what feel like seasons of hit after hit can also be seasons of great joy. It's important that we always weigh both sides, eliminate black-and-white thinking with either/ors, and welcome the word *and* into our vocabulary. At times when it felt I was the only one believing in my dreams, it gave me peace saying to myself, "It may seem like no one else is for me, *and* it doesn't matter because God and I are for me." See that shift?

We need to trust that God's ways are better than ours. Acceptance and trust go hand in hand. Once we can accept that God's will is always best, we can trust that when the times feel hard, he is working things out for us. Things will always work out, and when they haven't, remember that he's just not finished yet.

What is that deep desire that you've uncovered during your time reading this book? What do you know God is trying to encourage you to do but you're ignoring or resisting it because it feels so far out of reach? You might be in the messy middle today where you see no light at the end of the tunnel. Maybe you're in a desert season and you question every day you wake up whether this calling on your heart really is viable. Friend, I want you to remember that God wouldn't put a calling on your heart if he didn't believe you could live it out. If it's there, it means it's possible. You don't need anyone else's permission or belief in your dream. Go and bet on yourself!

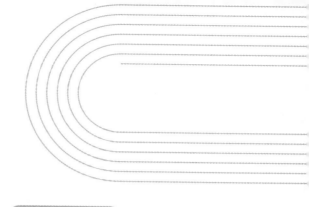

CHAPTER 8

Clear the Clutter
and Get Intentional

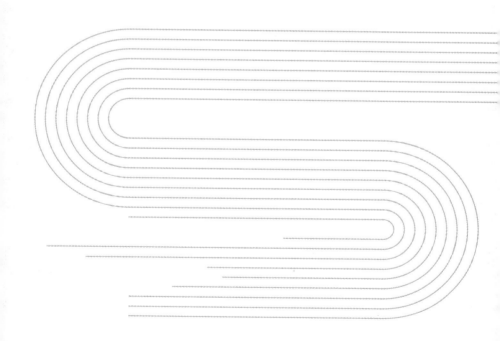

The best way to close this book is to go back to where we started, late winter 2020, the start of the pandemic and my forced quest to find intentionality. Those of us who are fortunate enough to live through the pandemic will agree that being contained with too many people or being alone with too much time to think absolutely forced us to find a way to take control of the environment around us. Because I couldn't control what was happening in the world, where our future was headed, and how little my kids would listen, I quickly realized that the one thing I could control was my mindset. And in order to best control the clutter in my mind, I needed to learn to better control the clutter around me.

I'll be honest with you. It all sort of began as a #parent oftheyear threat my husband and I would make when the kids didn't listen. I should preface this with just because I have therapist letters after my name doesn't mean I have all the answers. And to make myself feel better, my graduate school training was with adults, not kids, and when I did work with kids at the start of my career, they weren't my own, which makes the situation completely different. When dealing with your own, everything you learn goes out the window! So that parent-of-the-year phrase hubs and I started using when we wanted to yell and scream and lose our patience and felt powerless was this: "Okay, if you aren't listening, we will just start throwing toys in the trash." Not something I'm proud of, but it worked for about a week until our three-year-old (at the time), who is an old soul and wise beyond her years, caught on and began saying, "Fine, go ahead and throw them out." We never actually intended on throwing their toys out—maybe hiding them and putting the toys in a time-out for a while, but never throwing them away. But then it gave me a brilliant idea. If this clutter is swallowing my house whole and my kids have zero attachment to their toys too, why don't I just get rid of some of it? Not only was the clutter taking up space in my mind, but it also wasn't serving them and was causing unnecessary arguments among all of us.

Now, I wouldn't consider myself a full-blown minimalist, but what I know to be true is that when I have less clutter lingering around the house and fewer tabs open in my mind, I feel much more at peace and in better alignment. We live in a society today where bigger, better, and overabundance are symbols of success. We want the newest edition of the iPhone to have the best camera and most storage. We want the bigger house so we can stuff it with more meaningless crap we will never use. We want to outdo the neighbors' Christmas lights and blow-ups. Can we be honest, nonjudgmental adults here? I can't stand blow-ups. To me, they are a giant sensory overload, and I just don't get them! Anyway, this desire to create more inflated lives (no pun intended) has left our souls more deflated than anything. Depression and anxiety are at all-time highs. Living for instant gratification is destroying our impulse control, our gratitude, and our appreciation for the simple things in life. Why wait for your next wedding anniversary to get those luxurious bed linens you've been eyeing when you could have them delivered to your doorstep in three days or less? What made purchases exciting in the past was the entire process—working and saving up for those special items and then traveling to the store in hopes that they were in stock, always with the possibility of having to special order them. Which also forced us to be even more intentional with gift giving to make sure we had enough money saved with enough time to spare in case the store didn't stock the item. Today we sadly treat many things, opportunities, and relationships as disposable and no longer invest as much time, effort, and intentionality into our endeavors. And this leaves us only craving more, never quite feeling satisfied. Which is the complete opposite of what we are all going for: peace and fulfillment.

Take a moment to take inventory of your life. What physical, emotional, and relational clutter do you have hanging around? What possessions, patterns, and people deplete your time and energy and are no longer serving you? Despite the toys, we have a relatively simple life without a ton of things that need upkeep, except for our businesses. But we know many people who live a different lifestyle, and just to live it, they need to pour hours of time and much dedication into the upkeep of things such as boats, very large homes, pools, sports vehicles, collectors' items, and "everything in my storage unit." There is absolutely nothing wrong with these things, and kudos to you if you can manage them all. Maybe the clutter in your life has to do with your physical appearance—needing dozens of shoes, and outfits, and makeup or personal care items, and all the treatments and upkeep that come with nails, lashes, tinting, tweaking, plumping, or whatever else they do these days! Or maybe you're not devoting time and energy to physical things but to large friend groups and being a part of every social club, church group, outing, and party. At least four out of seven days of the week you are off to the next outing, and you honestly are beginning to feel tired. You feel emotionally depleted being so available and in so many people's problems and stories and can barely keep up with your own. Just like having nice things, social scenes can fill us up to an extent, but when we overdo it, they can rob us of the simplicity and intentionality that are available to us.

What if I told you that you can easily and quickly begin reversing a lifestyle of clutter? Now again, I'm not an expert on minimalism, but I've learned throughout the years that having more doesn't always bring more fullness and richness into our lives. I want to take some time before we part ways to address a topic I believe you'll keep coming back to. Maybe today you won't feel ready to begin the simplification process of living, but I guarantee someday you will. And this chapter will be here, waiting for you, nonjudgmentally with open arms. And if today you are like, "Kate, I am ready! I no longer want to feel weighed down by clutter," I am going to strike a match, pass it to you, and give you permission to burn the house down. All the physical, emotional, and relational clutter that has been weighing you down—let's remove it so that you can begin feeling lighter in your day-to-day, more intentional with the things and people you care most about, and, most importantly, filled up yourself. First, we will dive into why we hold on so tightly to physical, emotional, and relational clutter and the purpose that it serves. Then we will shine a light on what's available when we can metaphorically toss the junk mail and keep only what is of service to us. Then we will wrap up with some tangible steps you can take to clear the clutter from your life.

The Risk of False Comfort

Counterintuitively, clutter provides comfort. Each individual item, relationship, or aspect of our lives feels like home and a familiar place. Clutter provides not only comfort but also a false sense of hope for the future. "Maybe someday when I'm in need, she will be there for me. And even as unreliable as she is, if I let this relationship go, who will I have?" Or "Even though I can barely close the drawer, I should keep this to-go container because the lid might just turn up one of these days and I'll be able to use it again." Anyone else guilty of that one? These examples pop up constantly in our lives.

Although letting one strand of hair go down the shower drain seems innocent, over time, the hairs can cause a blockage and you're left in disbelief after unscrewing the drain and pulling out an enormous ball of your hair. "No way, that couldn't have all come from me. How did I let it get to this point? I never let more than one hair go down the drain at a time." The clutter, while providing a false sense of comfort, can catch up to us and emotionally haunt us if we aren't in a state of consistent mindfulness. Bigger picture and collectively, clutter leads to internal chaos, clouding our judgment. Clutter also quite literally holds us back from living the life of fullness God intends for us. It blocks us from the blessings and freedoms God has available for us. How good do you feel after you've done a big overhaul or spring cleaning and can sit back and look at how put-together your closet looks? You feel proud of yourself and can breathe a sigh of relief. I've also never heard someone say to me after the fact, "I wish I never donated those old dancing shoes I never wore" or "I wish I never released that toxic relationship that was keeping me up each night feeling used." Never have I ever heard regret from someone who let go of random things they no longer had use for, old habits that caused pain, and even people who were no longer life-giving to them. So can we just pause and take that in? There is a very high chance that if you release the clutter you've been holding on to, you might just end up feeling lighter, more fulfilled, and more focused on what matters most to you in the future.

Now let's take a moment for a little exercise. Close your eyes and picture the items, thoughts, and people that are clogging up your energy, your space, your joy right now. Envision releasing them one by one, releasing the weight, experiencing a newfound level of comfort you never knew existed. Now hold on to that vision. How would clearing the clutter change your life, the way you see things, and the way you treat and interact with what's surrounding you right now?

When I engage in this exercise, I first envision my closet and having only a few items in it that I love with the freedom to not feel guilt each time I don't choose the things that have been taking up space for years because they just aren't quite fitting right now. I think about having only a handful of close friends to text and chat with over the phone rather than having small-talk conversations with people I no longer feel attached and connected to but who are taking time away from the people I truly desire to communicate with. I think about my home and no longer being tempted to yell at my kids because everywhere I walk I step on a LEGO part or slip on an item from their never-ending dress-up bin. I envision them loving and respecting the few toys they have and not feeling overwhelmed and overstimulated by a sensory overload of toys in every corner of our home. I think about the ease of having many decisions made automatically for me so that I can put the energy into the decisions that are most important in my job, requiring the highest attention to detail. This is what clearing the mental and physical clutter looks like for us. Once we can release the false sense of comfort clutter has provided us with, we can begin to experience a freedom and an intentionality like we never have before, which then allows us to live fully in alignment.

Before I share my opinion of what releasing the clutter can open up for you, let's start with the truth of God's Word and what he has promised us for thousands of years. Hold on to your seat. This may surprise you, but the Bible has *a lot* to say about clearing the clutter! Let's start with some of my absolute favorite verses, Isaiah 43:18–19, in which God clearly promises newness and provision when we can release the things of the past: "Remember not the former things, nor consider the things of old. Behold, I am doing a new thing; now it springs forth, do you not perceive it? I will make a way in the wilderness and rivers in the desert." And then in Philippians 3:13–14, he reminds us that by forgetting the past and forging ahead, we will be led to what he has available for us: "But one thing I do: forgetting what lies behind and straining forward to what lies ahead, I press on toward the goal for the prize of the upward call of God in Christ Jesus."

Letting Go of Physical Holds to Gain Freedom

So first of all, we need to begin within our homes. "But as for me and my household, we will serve the Lord" (Josh. 24:15 NIV). We need to instill these mindsets and habits within the home, making it a steady and consistent place for intentional living. When we can get our partners, roommates, kids, even pets on board with the importance of living life to the fullest, we will eliminate unneeded frustration. We can tell someone a million times to do something, but when we model and show them how it's done, that is when the lesson is instilled.

As I'm on my own journey of intentionality, I am hoping that these little habits and mindsets will stick with my kids and influence their decisions regarding valuing the possessions, patterns, and people around them. We have tried really hard to model respecting what's within our home, even to the meals that we eat. We do this by showing gratitude by blessing each meal and reminding our children how fortunate we are to have the choice to be picky eaters. Whenever a new toy or item enters our home, we ask our girls to choose a current item to give to someone else. We are trying to teach them that it is just as blessed, if not more, to give than to receive. We also want to discourage attachment to material things, as they will not stay with us forever. Matthew 6:19–21 says it perfectly: "Do not store up for yourselves treasures on earth, where moths and vermin destroy, and where thieves break in and steal. But store up for yourselves treasures in heaven, where moths and vermin do not destroy, and where thieves do not break in and steal. For where your treasure is, there your heart will be also" (NIV). And by modeling unattachment to toys and blankies, we are trying to instill inner confidence and comfort in what God's Word says.

Practicing unattachment as adults is just as important! Ever known someone who has a major shopping addiction, continuing to buy new things in hopes they will fill some major void in their life, whether it be loneliness or lack of self-esteem? And they feel as though once they can physically have what they desire, they will experience security and comfort. However, acquiring more things ends up being counterproductive in a sense, giving false hope (again), robbing us of our hard-earned money, and leaving us feeling less comforted when we realize how little joy those things actually bring us. And this is why unattachment to possessions is crucial. When we can feel at home no matter our circumstances and not require certain items for comfort, we find there is a freedom and lightness available that we never knew existed.

I remember as a kid being so tightly attached to my things that if I went to a sleepover missing the tie to my robe or my purple hair scrunchie or if I had packed clean underwear with the wrong day of the week printed on them for the next day, I would quickly become bent out of shape! Imagine that! Today my husband jokes when we go on vacation because I often underpack and forget many of the essentials, typically including underwear. But to be honest, it's not because I am careless. I just no longer put value on needing everything to be perfect and can feel at peace and at home even if I lost my luggage and had only the clothes on my back.

How attached are you to your material possessions? Could you feel at peace if all of them were stripped away, or is this something you would like to work on?

Making Margin for Magic

Ever envy those in your life who don't have every minute of the day mapped out and can say yes to spontaneous dinner plans? This is something I really struggle with, not being intentional enough to have margin and envying those who are good at it. I wouldn't consider myself jealous of others' things or successes. However, when it comes to witnessing those who create margin for spontaneous road trips or even those who don't check their watch every five minutes to make sure they get back in time to the sitter, I see this as a short-coming for me and something I have to and will continue to nurture and develop. If you know anything about the Ennea-gram, I, as an Enneagram 3, have control over my schedule and how my time is used as rigidly as you've ever witnessed before. Trust me, I have come a long way over the years, but I am still asking God for grace and patience in this area. I'm not proud of it, but I can often relate to the priest and the Levite in the story of the good Samaritan. Luke 10:31 tells the story of a man who was lying on the side of a road and was ignored by travelers passing by him. At separate times, a priest and a Levite passed by this man in need, and rather than stopping to help him, they intentionally ignored him, walked to the other side of the road, and continued on their separate journeys, so fixated on their destinations.

This story always stings a bit because, like the priest, the Levite, and potentially others who most likely walked right by this man, I can get so fixated on my mission that I don't allow any margin for magic. Am I the only one? Or can any of you relate? Rather than turning your computer off to take a ten-minute walk around the block with your husband, you tell him, "Maybe tomorrow." Or rather than having a spontaneous coffee date with the bestie you haven't seen in months, you feel pulled to go home and follow through with your plan to finally deep clean the kitchen.

I know you probably get it. We pack our lives with so much, leaving very little room for the magic of life. But have you ever been really brave and paused or pushed off what you had hoped to accomplish to relish in the beauty of life with someone you love? How did that feel? Was it worth it, or did you regret it after? Here's the truth. When it's someone important to you, you most likely will not regret it. Or when you know that pausing your own plans to do a good deed made a difference in someone else's life, maybe even the life of a perfect stranger, you probably won't regret it either. If anything, you might receive a sense of satisfaction witnessing what little negative impact that time spent had on what needed to get done. Each and every time, I am truly amazed how easily I can shift things or how what I thought was necessary was really unnecessary. When we allow flexibility in our schedules and with those around us, we can welcome in a new freedom and level of fulfillment we never knew existed.

Releasing Emotional Pain

Mark 11:25 says, "And whenever you stand praying, forgive, if you have anything against anyone, so that your Father also who is in heaven may forgive you your trespasses." I can't tell you how many times in the last few years I have spent sleepless nights replaying situations, typically in my business, that have left me feeling used, angry, bitter, confused, and a slew of other emotions. I am really good at keeping business just business, but often when someone is distrustful or misleading or majorly drops the ball, it can be hard to just let go and let God. My human nature wants to control and fix and tell them how wrong they were. But the one thing I've learned throughout the years is that often, silence or choosing to walk away is the single most brave and impactful thing you can do to signal to the individual that you are not engaging in their shenanigans or wasting a breath over them. And in addition to this being the most impactful move you can make to influence them, it's hands down the best thing you can do for yourself.

I think back to my days in college, way before social media, and how empowered I felt after blocking phone numbers of toxic people in my life or the one time I actually changed my cell phone number after leaving an unhealthy relationship. In these instances, I declared to myself, "This person has hurt me, and I am no longer allowing their toxicity to rent space in my mind. I am cutting ties, blessing and releasing them, and beginning again from a clean slate. I am forgiving them for the pain they caused me and allowing that pain to be a marker of what I don't want in my next relationship." I wouldn't pray for them to fall and break their ankle, although that would often be my initial thought, but rather I would pray for God to reveal where their hearts needed healing and use this parting to grow and develop them.

I know we talked quite a bit about choice in this book. I quite honestly think we forget how powerful choice really is. God has given us the choice either to hold a grudge, along with pain and bitterness, or to bless and release the space a particular person was taking up in our hearts and minds. I've learned that in so many of these unhealthy situations, nothing about the situation ever changes. However, my life changes because I've shifted my perspective. After realizing how much time and energy it would take to fight when someone didn't hold up their end of a bargain, I blessed and released the situation. When a client was delinquent on payments after giving every story in the world about how although they make half a million, they can't scrape together enough to pay me, what did I do? I blessed and released. Even in the times when we aren't proud of something we did or said or how we reacted to someone, we must still forgive, bless, and release—yes, even ourselves. God talks a ton about forgiveness in the Bible. I believe it's because of the power and stronghold it can truly have over our lives. When we release painful situations, we open our hearts to blessing and goodness and freeness. Giving yourself permission to feel good is the single best decision you can make when you are prone to holding on to emotional clutter. Take a moment to ponder these questions:

1. What have you been holding on to today just to prove a point?

2. What have you been holding on to today because you know you're right and the other person is wrong?

3. How would it feel to just raise the white flag and acknowledge that the situation occurred, was painful, and impacted you, but you will no longer allow it to have a stronghold over you one more second of your life?

So now that we know why, as humans, we are so intricately connected to our internal and external clutter, what is possible for us and actually waiting for us when we can release and let it go, it's now time to get to the good stuff. I want to show you how simple it really is to start releasing the possessions, patterns, and people who aren't providing life and fullness and abundance in your life.

Determine Wants versus Needs

By learning simple mindsets and behaviors that can be used immediately, you will find it much easier to adapt to the more intricate ones later. So let's begin with the easiest tip first. Years ago when leading a Bible study with my bestie, we decided that rather than doing a traditional white elephant or secret Santa exchange, we would do a wants versus needs exchange. Now, this was totally her brilliant idea, as I'm not quite as creative with gift giving. We were all broke grad school students, so our max was $10 a person. We asked group members to write on an index card a list of things they needed that were under five dollars and a list of wants that were under five dollars. This gift exchange ended up serving three very specific purposes. First, it was fun to bless someone with a gift and also fun to receive a blessing. Second, we were given something that we needed that was maybe not so fun for us to spend our own money on, like Band-Aids or a new spatula or a pack of hair elastics. And last, it gave us the opportunity to get super creative and envision a small gift that would spark joy. So often we put pressure on ourselves and think that in order for a gift to be worthy, it needs to cost a lot of money. Well, in this instance, people found creative ways to give really special gifts for not a lot of money. Some asked for a book they really wanted that was secondhand.

Some people made homemade gifts that cost much less than purchased ones—for example, a beautiful wool winter hat! It was hands down the best gift exchange I ever participated in, and it taught me a huge lesson: to treat every purchase as a need versus want.

This completely shifted my mindset around money and acquiring things I really didn't need. It also taught me to be more intentional with my wants. From that day forward, I began to look at items with more appreciation. Gifts began to feel more cherished, as I knew they would serve a purpose. This shift has also saved us a ton of money over the years. I can decide whether brand-new is necessary or getting something secondhand would make more sense. For instance, the last car we purchased was a need, as our family was growing. So getting a bigger vehicle was necessary, but was purchasing a brand-new vehicle a need or a want? It certainly was a want! And by realizing that in our current financial season a brand-new car was simply a want, we saved close to twenty thousand dollars by purchasing a vehicle with 17,000 miles on it. Not only were the savings great, but we also had peace of mind with a monthly payment that wouldn't stretch us thin.

The same goes for so many other items in our lives! Often we buy something to use for vacation or a move or a season of our kids' lives when someone we know down the street has that exact item sitting in storage that they can lend us for that short bit of time. Yes, it takes a little more intention and effort to ask around, but borrowed items will leave you feeling less weighed down financially and won't take up space being stored in your home. As soon as our girls outgrow clothing, shoes, toys, or any of the kid paraphernalia, I ask around to see who wants to take or who wants to borrow (if we will need it back in the future).

Learning to live life from a place of asking yourself two simple questions will help you clear the clutter and will enrich your quality of living that much more. So next time you go to make a purchase, ask yourself, "Is this a want or a need? And what makes most sense in the financial season I am in?"

Don't Try to Be Superwoman

Okay, here is your next tip for clearing the clutter so you can have more mental clarity and margin for the goodness of life: *Never* keep anything in your head. This is probably the most simplistic tip you will get from me in this book, but it's über important. Our lives are already cluttered. You are not superwoman. Write down every single thing. Don't ever count on your brain to remember dates, events, preferences, shopping lists, meetings, etc. And especially if you've had kids, baby brain is a real thing. I often forget what or even if I ate lunch some days. If something is important or needs to be done, write it in a planner, in a notebook, on a Post-it Note, on a clean page in the notes section of your phone, or in some type of digital planner or task system that can hold life together for you so that you don't need to. I can't tell you how many people I know who say, "Oh, I don't need to write anything down. I have the best memory." Well, kudos to you if this is you. But imagine how much better life could be if you could also write it all down and take that pressure off yourself to remember. Please start today.

Make a Daily Clean Sweep

It's important that we take a daily inventory of the mental or physical clutter that no longer serves us. Take consistent inventory of relationships, habits, or possessions that truly are no longer serving you. And if you can immediately get rid of them, do it! If you aren't quite sure if it's time to part ways, try this instead. Commit to a fast, as we discussed earlier in the book. Fasting doesn't have to be reserved just for something like anxiety or major healing. It can be used for anything that is keeping you from living fully and intentionally.

After becoming quite obsessed with checking the news, publications, opinion accounts, and social media during the monumental year of a pandemic and extreme social and political unrest, I realized how life-sucking it really was. In some ways, checking and educating myself, having the facts, and being able to formulate my own take on things gave me peace, but they also led to an obsession of wanting to be up-to-date and on top of it all. I tried cutting back my consumption of news each day, but it wasn't quite enough. So I completely cut the news out of my life for thirty days. During that period of time, whenever I was tempted to check the news, I filled my life with God's Word or uplifting words or connected with a loved one. After a few days, I felt convicted to lay down more and decided to add ten more days. After forty full days news free, during an election, I can honestly say my life felt so much richer, less on edge, and more in control than ever before. It was one of the best things I did that year, and by getting a taste of what life could be like sans distractors, I now automatically guard my mind when it comes to what I put in it. If you can implement this simple skill of clearing the clutter in your life each day, I promise you that so much blessing, goodness, and peace will have space to enter in.

Say It to Believe It

This tip will require a little more self-discipline. It can feel rewarding to do things like cut clutter from our lives, but adding in things can be a bit more of a challenge. But now that you have opened up a bit of space by clearing the clutter, you really have no excuse not to find margin to add this next activity to your life: Practice daily affirmations. I believe in affirmations like no other, yet I find it challenging to recite a new one daily. So I simplify by focusing on one affirmation each month.

So come up with a list of intentions or beliefs you would like to embrace and write them down. You can even take ten to fifteen minutes right now, brainstorm twelve, one for each month, and boom, you are done! Each month hang that affirmation in a place or multiple places where it will be visible to you and say it daily. One of my favorites is "The less I actually have, the more fulfilling my life feels." But you can use even simpler ones—for example, "Quality over quantity," "NO," "Less = more." I can't tell you how impactful simple words and phrases can be in helping us stick to our goals and live with intentionality.

Cast a Vision

Finally, I want you to spend time envisioning where you desire to be. Whenever you catch yourself succumbing to the swirl of life again, pause and spend a few minutes visualizing what you want your life to be like and how you would feel if you could achieve the level of peace you desire. What would this look like? Grab a journal and jot down what comes up for you. Close your eyes and really sit in this vision.

Next, remind yourself that it's currently available to you by just slowing down and clearing a bit more out. When I get into a mental swirl and do this exercise, it typically leads me to a garbage bag and my trusted planner. I begin releasing more of the things that are readily available for me to release in that very moment. Each and every time I take the time that I feel I don't have for this exercise and clear the clutter, I open up time and space in my life and, in turn, feel a million times more grounded and peaceful afterward.

I hope you will revisit these practices often and that you will be amazed at how significant they can be for creating more peace, balance, and simplicity in your life. Remember, God didn't design us to live a boundary-less life filled up with people, things, and beliefs that aren't life-giving. Remember Matthew 6:21: "For where your treasure is, there your heart will be also." Meditate on and arm yourself with this truth.

CONCLUSION

Tying It All Together

Let's admit that when we are in the swirl of life with no end in sight, in the clouded muck, it can be pretty tempting to make feel-good-in-the-moment decisions from this place of desperation and brokenness. It's easy to embody absolutes such as "There is no way out," "I am going to fail," and "This is too hard to bear" rather than looking to God's Word and trusting what he tells us is really for us. I was there, friends, completely hopeless and desperate to cling to anything that would potentially serve as a quick fix to pull me out of the desert season. As I edit this book over and over again, I find it difficult to articulate in these pages the extent of pain I endured that year because of where I am today. That despair feels like lifetimes away, and guess what? It can feel that way for you too. In the year 2020, God wiped the muck from my eyes and replaced it with his clear and perfect 20/20 vision.

This process of drawing the line, setting limits, trusting yourself, trusting your heavenly Father, decluttering what no longer serves you, and so on will take hard work. You're going to need to intentionally uncover your blind spots, and in doing so, you might need help from an outsider. You'll need to learn new patterns of thinking and practice them until they become second nature. You'll need to break away from the potentially prideful plans you had for your life and grab hold of the potentially humble and what may feel like minuscule plans God has for you. You might need to find a professional therapist to continue the work with you and hold you accountable. In order to cultivate a life of true fulfillment and alignment, boundary lines will need to be drawn. And in that process, you may risk losing it all. But believe me when I say it's worth every last ugly cry. Often, losing it all is the only way to rebuild.

As I type these words exactly one year from the story that started our journey together, today all the painful pieces seem to make sense. What feels clearer than ever is that God is an intentional Father. He is intentional in his healing, taking each of our broken pieces—fear, uncertainty, disappointment, loss, insecurity, shame, and so on—and mending them back together. He doesn't just put them back together to create the former vessel. He takes the pieces and refines, remolds, and then fuses them back together to form a brand-new, whole vessel. I am still the Kate we started with, but from the loss, disappointment, and stretching that I endured, I can now see the world, my loved ones, and those around me through a completely different lens. God has replaced my blinders, such as my selfish plans and ambitions, with a humility to serve, trust, and lean on him like never before. Here's the thing though. When you are in the swirl of life, you are doing your best. What you see is all you know. What you're experiencing may actually be aligned for you in that season. But God always has more. He doesn't just want you to stay aligned where you are. He wants you to continually learn and step into a new level of alignment.

As we wrap up our time together, I feel I have a duty to share these next words with you.

Above all else, go directly to the source, Jesus Christ. It can be so tempting to read every self-help book under the sun or process our pain with those around us until the cows come home, but, ultimately, peace, fulfillment, abundance, and alignment can only and simply be found in his Word. After working with women for over a decade on uncovering their purpose and making their goals a reality, I can confidently say that the skills and tactics of the world will only get you so far. Don't get me wrong. They work, but only to an extent.

After mixing together all the ingredients to bake a decadent chocolate cake, you can quickly satisfy your craving by indulging in some cake batter. Most of us would agree that raw batter is delicious, providing us with that quick fix while we anxiously pace the kitchen, checking the oven and waiting for the finished product. Although raw batter can satisfy that in-the-moment craving, it has the potential to leave us hunched over running to the bathroom if we aren't careful, yet we still partake. The wait feels brutal, like eternity, to get the finished product. But it has to go through the fire. It needs time—time to bake and then time to cool. The process takes self-control and patience. Well, friends, that oven is our heavenly Father and that batter is our world. Quick fixes will only get us so far, but braving the pain and taking the longer road will lead us not only to the source that will satisfy us but also to eternity. So as you go out on this journey to continue your search for alignment, make sure you continually keep God close and guard your heart from what might provide you with a temporary fix.

So today I ask myself, "How is life different than it was a year ago?" First and foremost, I boldly surrendered. I raised my white flag after stubbornly and pridefully fighting against God's plans for several months and said, "God, show me your ways. Take my life (again) and place me on the path you want me on," which ended up being home. As I write this today, March 2021, this is the girls' first full week back in four-day-a-week school. We are right back to where we started a year ago, but life has completely shifted. My old life and desires feel so foreign, and my current lines feel so clear. Here are some things that have changed for me since I surrendered and drew my line:

- Unhealthy business ventures have come to an end.
- Relationships that once felt toxic have since been restored.
- My worth is no longer tied to the number of books I sell.
- I no longer censor what I have to say in fear of offending someone.
- Prideful desires in my career have been pushed aside and humility has entered.
- I have an unshakable confidence knowing that I am a child of God, which is a birthright that does not need to be earned by striving.

I want to end how we started our time together, sharing God's beautiful promise of alignment when we can draw our own boundary lines.

The LORD is my chosen portion and my cup;
>   you hold my lot.
The lines have fallen for me in pleasant places;
>   indeed, I have a beautiful inheritance.
I bless the LORD who gives me counsel;
>   in the night also my heart instructs me.
I have set the LORD always before me;
>   because he is at my right hand, I shall not be
>   shaken.
Therefore my heart is glad, and my whole being
>   rejoices;
>   my flesh also dwells secure.
For you will not abandon my soul to Sheol,
>   or let your holy one see corruption.
You make known to me the path of life;
>   in your presence there is fullness of joy;
>   at your right hand are pleasures forevermore. (Ps.
>   16:5–11)

In order to step into this promise that is available for us, we need to be crystal clear on what our goals, desires, and dreams are by tuning in to God's voice. And the only way we can begin hearing from God is by silencing the noise. We need to slow down and begin releasing the things that no longer serve us and may even be toxic. We need to begin doing more of what fills our cup rather than pouring from our empty pitchers. We need to state and claim what we feel God has placed on our hearts, no matter how out of reach or impossible the dream may feel. We need to begin praying audacious prayers and believing for God-sized abundance in all areas of our lives, not because we deserve it but because it has already been written, even before our birth. And once we become so confident that God has indeed called us to live not just a mediocre, check-off-my-to-do-list life but a fulfilled kind of life, we will begin stepping into a place of full alignment.

Remember, friends, our God is a big God! He gives us strength to pull through the unimaginable. We cannot do it through our own strength but through his. At bedtime each night, I pray words of power over the girls: "Help them be strong, courageous, resilient." Then I end the prayer with, "And help them get right back up every time they fall. Amen." It's not if but when. Pain is inevitable, and the sooner we can embrace the duality that life can still be joyful in the midst of suffering, the sooner it will feel easier. And remember, we always have a choice. We can choose for life to feel hard by resisting the current, or we can choose alignment by cultivating humility and surrendering and allowing God to swoop in and take over. And the sooner we can grasp that we do have a choice and release control of outcomes, the sooner we can begin living the life he designed for us—a life of ultimate freedom, fulfillment, peace, and alignment. Now, as we part ways, let's begin this next chapter of life by drawing the line. Here is my prayer for you:

Lord, give them the confidence to know they are already strong, courageous, humble, resilient, and wise. Help them to see themselves as you see them. Help them to dream big dreams and give them discernment to know when and where to draw their boundary lines. And help them get right back up every time they fall. In Jesus's name, amen.

ACKNOWLEDGMENTS

I'd be lying if I said this time around was even half as strenuous as writing my first book. I'm not sure if it was having my first book under my belt or completely putting my trust in the Lord to give me the right words to say. Maybe it was simply me being so mentally drained from trying to say the right things to keep people liking me that I just stopped caring. Honestly, I think it was a little of each. The lessons I teach in this book are the exact lessons I was wrestling with during each step of the process. Each time something began to feel difficult, I examined it and asked myself why, and 99 percent of the time, it was because I was choosing to make it difficult because of my own doubts, insecurities, or people pleasing tendencies. Once I could identify this and snap out of it, I would tell myself, "My job is to model complete and unapologetic living in every step of my life." And by standing firm in this mission, the result was a writing process that felt easy because it was in complete alignment.

While growing and birthing our third sweet babe, Andrew Joseph, better known as Dreamy Drewey, I wrestled with the lesson of force versus flow. Specifically, in the last six weeks of my pregnancy, I was tested beyond belief, on the verge of forcing birth through induction just to alleviate back pain. During those long, grueling days, I reread my own words several times and remembered that when we let go of control and allow life to unfold God's way, it ends up being so much easier. And because I welcomed the pain in the waiting rather than forcing a faster outcome, I had the sweetest, fastest, and most magical unmedicated birth (not by choice!).

Andrew, my darling husband, what a wild eighteen months this has been for us. It was a rocky start, to say the least, going from spending mostly just weekends together to transforming our home into an inescapable three-ring circus. Not only did we learn to adapt, but better yet, we learned to enjoy and savor each moment, wild as they could be. I couldn't ask for a better partner in crime than you. Teamwork makes the dream work. Cheers to crazier dreams and bigger adventures!

Keely, I know I said this the last time, but I mean it. You are a GEM—one in a million. Not only have you championed me, but you have also been my voice of reason MANY times. I look forward to what the future brings in our journey together.

To the entire Baker team—it has been an honor to collaborate on a second book with you. Rebekah, thank you for believing in this book and helping me sort out the concept early on. You helped me birth a book I didn't even realize I had within me, which led me to the most life-giving lesson of 2021. Thank you also, Rebekah, for connecting me with Nicci, who felt like a writing therapist (yes, that should really be a thing!) and encouraged me to follow my intuition and not stray from alignment. Eileen, our brainstorm calls were always a highlight of my week. Olivia, thank you for helping with all the little details. And Laura, you nailed this cover design!

To all my girlfriends, family members, clients, and social media friends who cheered me on throughout this whole process—I truly couldn't do this on my own. Your love notes and words of encouragement are what kept me going!

Kate Crocco, MSW, LCSW, is a psychotherapist and business mindset coach who mentors female leaders around the globe. She has coached thousands of women through one-on-one, group, and mastermind programs, as well as through her Confident Ladies Club™ community. She is the host of a weekly podcast, *Thinking Like a Boss*, where she equips entrepreneurs to stop believing the lies holding them back from success and to begin believing the truth that they are capable of turning their dreams into their reality. A guest expert on numerous podcasts and telesummits, Kate has been quoted in publications including the *Huffington Post*, *Best Kept Self*, *SheKnows*, and *BlogHer*. Kate's mission is to empower women to go after their dreams by helping them break down the barriers that have been holding them back from greatness through lovingly challenging them to step in to the best version of themselves. Kate currently resides in New York with her husband, her three babes four and under, and her rescue pup, Turbo.

Connect with Kate

KATECROCCO.COM/PODCAST

  KateCrocco

Join
THE CONFIDENT LADIES CLUB
FACEBOOK COMMUNITY

THE CONFIDENT LADIES CLUB
with Kate Crocco

 @katecrocco   Thinking Like A Boss Podcast

Be part of a community of *supportive, heart-centered, miracle-working* lady bosses.

More from *Kate*

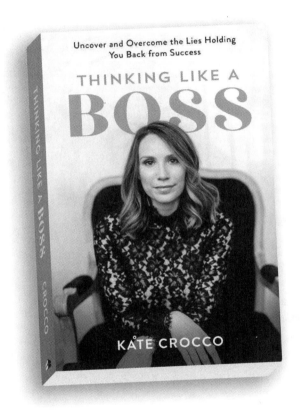

With plenty of inspiring true stories and actionable steps you can take—starting now—Kate Crocco exposes the twelve limiting beliefs that are holding you back from your true potential.

Connect with
BakerBooks
Relevant. Intelligent. Engaging.

Sign up for announcements about
new and upcoming titles at

BakerBooks.com/SignUp

@ReadBakerBooks